The Complete
Home Workshop

The Complete Home Workshop

David H. Jacobs, Jr.

TAB Books

Division of McGraw-Hill, Inc.

New York   San Francisco   Washington, D.C.   Auckland   Bogotá
Caracas   Lisbon   London   Madrid   Mexico City   Milan
Montreal   New Delhi   San Juan   Singapore
Sydney   Tokyo   Toronto

FIRST EDITION
FIRST PRINTING

© 1994 by **TAB Books**.
TAB Books is a division of McGraw-Hill, Inc.

Library of Congress Cataloging-in-Publication Data
Jacobs, David H.
   The complete home workshop / by David H. Jacobs, Jr.
     p. cm.
   Includes index.
   ISBN 0-07-032403-4 (pbk.)
   1. Workshops—Design and construction.   2. Workshops—Equipment and supplies. I. Title.
TT152.J33   1994
684—dc20   94-3091
                                                         CIP

Acquisitions editor: April Nolan
Editorial team: Joanne Slike, Executive Editor
              Lori Flaherty, Managing Editor
              Steve Bolt, Editor
Production team: Katherine G. Brown, Director
                Ollie Harmon, Coding
                Rose McFarland, Desktop Operator
                Toya Warner, Computer Illustrator
                Joann Woy, Indexer
Design team: Jaclyn J. Boone, Designer
            Brian Allison, Associate Designer
Cover design: Cindy Staub   HT1
Cover copy writer: Michael Crowner   0324034

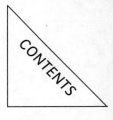

I want to thank a number of people for their enthusiastic support and continued encouragement throughout the course of writing this book. In addition, my family and I extend our most sincere gratitude to everyone who has assisted us in so many different ways to help make our multipurpose home workshop a reality.

I most appreciate the overall support provided by Jack Hori, senior vice president, and Roy Thompson, product marketing manager, for Makita USA, Inc. Throughout months of constant use in a huge variety of home construction endeavors, we have received rugged, reliable, and precision service from all of our Makita tools. My first-hand experience using many Makita products for all sorts of projects enables me to confidently and comfortably recommend that you outfit your new home workshop with Makita.

Much gratitude is extended to Francis Hummel, marketing director for The Stanley Works, for his continued support. We have used a wide range of Stanley hand tools for all kinds of home improvement and workshop-finishing tasks. Each tool has performed as expected every time. Likewise, our workshop's Stanley steel door was a snap to install and the Stanley Goldblatt drywall finishing tools made those related endeavors much easier to accomplish. For hand tools, hardware, and doors, I recommend Stanley.

I must thank David Martel, marketing manager for Central Purchasing, Inc. (Harbor Freight Tools), for his assistance and support. Along with Makita and Stanley products, the Harbor Freight Tools catalog is packed with pages of interesting and useful home improvement tools and supplemental products. Call Harbor Freight Tools toll free to request a catalog.

We are very happy and most satisfied with our Eagle window and door products, and want to thank Tom Tracy, advertising manager, and John Stearns, general manager for Eagle's Bellevue, Washington window center, for their genuine interest and support. Our Eagle windows and door units were easy to install and operate very smoothly. If your home-improvement projects or new workshop endeavors include plans for new windows and doors, I recommend Eagle.

Our thanks go to Tom Marsh, vice president of marketing, and Daryl Hower, business manager, for Leslie-Locke, Inc., for their help with our roof window, attic ventilation, and heat-ducting needs. Installing Leslie-Locke products is easy and straightforward. They are most efficient and attractive, too.

Kohler was our first choice for bathroom accessories and I want to thank Peter Fetterer, from Kohler's public affairs department for all of his help and timely assistance. Kohler's range of quality bathroom products is most impressive and you will be delighted at the variety of styles and colors offered.

In addition to those already mentioned, I very much want to thank the following people and the companies they represent for their ongoing support and professional assistance: Betty Talley and Jeff Barnes for American Tool Companies; Hilarie Meyer for Campbell Hausfeld; Dave Shanahan for Keller Ladders; Rob Guzikowski for Simpson Strong-Tie Connector Company; Mr. Dana Young for PanelLift Telpro; Victor Lopez for Behr Process Corporation; Greg Hook for Plumb Shop (Brass-Craft); Kim Garretson and Rich Sharp for DAP, Inc.; Jim Schmiedeskamp and Phyllis Camesano for Owens-Corning; Matt Ragland for Empire Brush; Mike Cunningham for General Cable Company (Romex); Mario Mattich for Leviton; Ruth Tudor for NuTone; Bob McCully for SIMKAR (Power Products Company); Bill Cork for Plano Molding Company; Dick Warden for Structron Corporation; Marty Sennett for DuPont Tyvek; Beth Wintermantel for Weiser Lock; Peter Wallace for McGuire-Nicholas; Timm Locke for Western Wood Products Association; Maryann Olson for American Plywood Association; Don Meucci for Cedar Shake and Shingle Bureau; Tina Alexiess for Autodesk Retail Products; Patricia McGirr for Alta Industries; Jim Brewer for Freud; Sue Gomez for Zircon Corporation; Philip Martin for Häfele America Co.; Jeff Bucar for Halo Lighting; Matthew Smith for U.S. Ceramic Tile; and Jim Richeson for Sta-Put Color Pegs.

Our good friends Jim Yocum, Brian Lord, and Bob Greer spent a lot of time helping us put together our new workshop, and my family and I thank them for their energetic and always entertaining assistance. Likewise, we thank their wives Pamela,

Vicki, and Diane for their patience. Thanks to my ol' buddy Keith Rieber and to Josh Pearson, John Gittings, Steve Hayes, Ken Whitehair, Ryan Stearns, and Steve Emmanuels.

Van and Kim Nordquist of Photographic Designs did another outstanding job printing up hundreds of pictures to perfection and I am grateful for their expertise and patience.

I appreciate the experienced thoughts about workshop layouts passed along by Dennis Fortier, shop foreman for Logan Lumber Company's cabinet shop, as well as, the consideration and building suggestions offered by Scott Wakeford and Al Davis from Mercer Island's Building Department. Thanks also for the patience of our neighbors Dariush and Lisa Parvin for graciously enduring our construction noise and activities.

Having a professional tradesperson in the family sure came in handy, and we are grateful for all of the work accomplished by certified electrician and son-in-law Steve Brown. The rest of the family also pitched in wherever possible. So, thank you Nicholas, Luke, Bethany, Ashleigh, Matthew, Adam, Brittany, Courtney, Kirsten, Terri, Whitney, Tyler, Michele, Jake, Shannon, and Joey. And a big thank you to my wife, Janna, for her ever optimistic help in the workshop and office.

Finally, I want to thank Kim Tabor, April Nolan, and Julie Langas from TAB/McGraw-Hill for all of their continued encouragement, assistance, and support. Their enthusiasm and professionalism is most refreshing.

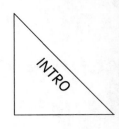

Y OUR FIRST thoughts of putting together a genuine workshop should be filled with delight. After all, do-it-yourselfers treasure puttering around and fixing things or spending quality time building home-improvement projects. A tool in every place, a place for every tool, and room in which to actually maneuver. That would be great!

It is exciting to think about enormous buildings with spacious assembly areas, large workbenches with lots of tool storage, and practically an entire home-improvement center's inventory tucked away in convenient store rooms.

Unfortunately, for most of us, reality eventually takes over and we must come to grips with the fact that our workshop resources probably will be limited to a basement, a vacant bedroom, the garage, the carport area, or a small outbuilding. Nevertheless, you can put together a viable home workshop if you take the time to carefully plan an organized work center that is set up for the types of tasks you expect to normally undertake.

Woodworkers who favor small projects will simply need room for a scroll saw, a bench sander, and a small storage area. Do-it-yourself homeowners regularly faced with typical appliance repairs, cabinet building, and other large jobs will need wide open spaces for maneuvering.

Know your plan

What are your workshop resources and how much room do you really need? Could a different arrangement of tools, equipment, and workbenches offer more working room? Would a storage cabinet in an open basement corner free up other spaces occupied by power tools or wood stock? How about a separate combination storage cabinet and fold-down work table for lightweight woodworking or home-repair tasks?

For those contemplating the construction of a dedicated home workshop, plan to spend lots of time thinking about your layout of workbenches, equipment, storage cabinets, electrical and compressed-air outlets, lights, switches, windows, doors, skylights, and conveniences such as a refrigerator, telephone, sound system, intercom, and so on.

A professional mechanic by trade, Mike Holiman is an avid do-it-yourself homeowner who thoroughly enjoys participating as the chief mechanic for a sprint-car crew. Before construction began on his home-based, 24-x-36-foot workshop, he spent a year planning how he would set it up to best accommodate both his automotive and do-it-yourself home-improvement endeavors. Even though a great amount of time was put into planning, he still makes occasional adjustments to improve workspace convenience.

Dennis Fortier is the shop foreman at Logan Lumber Company's cabinet shop. Although he has been a professional craftsman for decades, he still manages to find new ways of reorganizing the shop to improve overall work operations. He might reduce distances from tools to stock storage, locate certain tools or pieces of equipment closer to or further away from others, or install cabinets or shelves more strategically.

Chances are, once you have your shop finished and outfitted, you will also find yourself moving things around to better accommodate projects and convenience. With that in mind, take time to actually measure your table saw, radial arm saw, planer, jointer, shaper, drill press, and other workshop accessories. Transfer the dimensions onto graph paper and design your workshop to scale. Draw in workbenches, windows, storage units, and everything else you would like to have in there.

Draw, erase, and draw again. Sooner or later, a definitive plan will fall into place and you'll be ready to tackle plumbing, electrical, drywall, pegboard, painting, and other workshop finishing tasks.

A perfect workshop layout for one person might not suit the needs or desires of another. Likewise, not everybody enjoys working on the same types of projects. Tool, workbench, and storage needs differ. Therefore, about the only common workshop denominators are the basics: walls, lights, power, storage, and so on. *The Complete Home Workshop* focuses on ways to accomplish the fundamentals and then offers suggestions on how you might go about designing overall floor plans that best suit your needs and desires.

This book is designed to give you a wide range of practical information regarding a host of home workshop necessities, accessories, and options. Certainly not envisioned to be the last word in workshop design, it is my hope you will learn how to accomplish a variety of tasks that will, in turn, provide you with the confidence to undertake endeavors that result in a safe, comfortable, and efficient home workshop.

Involve your family

Home improvement projects and the setting up of home workshops should be structured so that family members are given opportunities to participate. Involvement, of course, should be commensurate with each person's age and physical abilities. Younger family members might be put in charge of cleanup and hand-tool retrieval, while older ones could assist in actual hands-on construction.

Realistic family participation should result in a true sense of shared self-satisfaction. Novice do-it-yourselfers in your family can be taught all sorts of things first-hand, from the names and terms of various tools and building materials to how home components are actually constructed and put together. In addition, you might be pleasantly surprised at the quality of work they produce.

During the construction of our workshop project, Luke and Nick (ages nine and seven) turned out to be two of my best helpers. They retrieved nails, tools, extension cords, boards, and all sorts of stuff. When my adult helpers and I took breaks or quit for the day, these enthusiastic boys tidied up our work areas like real professionals! After just a couple of days instruction about storing things and lessons about safety, I didn't have to say a word. Luke and Nick knew exactly where to store things, how to stack lumber neat and secure, where to dispose of construction debris, and how to coil extension cords so the cords would pay out evenly the next time we needed them.

Safety instructions

While construction work is underway, younger family members should be directed to watch from safe distances. Away from areas where they could get hurt, observers should generally be close enough to hear instructions for tasks you need them to do or conversations about what you are building or installing.

Most people find it is easiest to learn how to do things by first watching others complete tasks before they attempt the same. While your family works with and watches you, be sure to stress the importance of personal safety and then practice what you preach.

Be sure to position electrical cords out of the way. Always use safety goggles, hearing protection devices, the saw's protective guard, a push block to move wood past the saw blade, a sawdust collector, and a roller stand to support wood passed by the end of the saw's table.

Even with the saw's protective guard in place, a table saw poses the dangerous threat of kicking wood back out toward an operator at unbelievable speeds and with enough power to force wood through walls.

When novice do-it-yourselfers are taught from the beginning to wear personal safety devices, properly adjust tool guards, and operate tools and equipment according to manufacturer's recommendations, they will generally employ these safe work habits during every workshop and home-improvement endeavor. This is a fundamental goal that cannot be overemphasized.

Teaching family members at any early age about the importance of on-the-job safety should accustom them to a constant awareness of personal workshop safety. This will lead to a lifetime of automatic use of personal protective devices every time a project is started.

Driving and pulling nails using tools designed for such jobs is one of the first things young do-it-yourselfers will probably learn. Insist pupils wear safety goggles and follow common-sense safety practices. Demonstrate how properly employed leverage can make such jobs easier by placing a block of wood next to partially extracted nails to improve hammer or bar pulling power and help users maintain better control over such operations.

Cutting wood with a hand saw is another fundamental job novices must learn through practice. Again, follow basic workshop safety rules by mandating the use of safety goggles, teaching inexperienced do-it-yourselfers how to properly secure wood to sturdy sawhorses or stands, and making sure that nearby power equipment is bolted down to stands or workbenches and disconnected from power sources.

You must be keenly aware of what might be lurking behind wall surfaces anytime home-improvement work involves cutting out sections of existing walls.

Initial stages of putting together new home workshops will undoubtedly result in having to work with limited power supplies, at least until all electrical alterations have been completed. Problems will include a lack of sufficient, safe lighting. Portable halogen lights that put out a great deal of light could be powered from a heavy-duty extension cord stretched to a neighbor's house. If need be, especially during major service panel renovations, consider using a power generator.

Far too many do-it-yourself homeowners suffer preventable injuries as a result of unsafe ladder practices. Reaching too far off of ladder sides, standing on ladder tops, placing ladders on unstable surfaces, leaning ladders against buildings at awkward angles, and failing to keep rungs or steps clean are a few of the more common mistakes that generally lead to ladder accidents. Always be 100 percent certain that extension ladders are never raised near any power lines or other electrical components. Electricity from wires will short out through a ladder that makes contact with the wires, and could then electrocute someone holding onto the ladder.

If the surface your ladder must rest upon is uneven, use a device designed specifically to level the ladder legs or block up surface areas with 2 × 4s and wide pieces of plywood. On slick wood surfaces, nail a block of wood at ladder bases to prevent the ladder legs from sliding out and away from the building. The Keller Ladder Company recommends 75½ degrees as the proper climbing angle for extension ladders.

Accomplish this angle by setting ladder bases one-quarter of the ladder's working length away from the support or wall the ladder top will rest against. When gaining access to roofs, make sure ladders extend at least 3 feet above roof edges. As a rule of thumb, ladders are close to proper climbing angles when users can stand with their toes touching ladder bases and then grab ladder sides with their hands while arms are extended out.

Clean and uncluttered work areas help to keep them accident free. In lieu of awkwardly maneuvering around obstacles while involved with workshop finishing tasks, take time to relocate obstructions and sweep up piles of sawdust and wood scrap. Better yet, let your helpers tidy up. Make sure all power tools are unplugged and placed in safe locations before allowing youngsters into work areas for cleanup duties.

Along with wearing personal safety devices and following manufacturers recommendations for safe tool and equipment usage, have a fully serviceable first-aid kit and fire extinguisher on hand.

First-aid kits should include adhesive bandages, gauze pads, gauze rolls, tape, and scissors as a minimum inventory. Fully loaded kits are available through safety supply outlets, medical supply stores, and some home-improvement centers.

Multipurpose fire extinguishers with an ABC rating are suitable for Class A (ordinary combustibles such as wood and paper), Class B (flammable liquids), and Class C (electrical) fires. Home workshops should be outfitted with at least one unit rated at 2A:10B:C. Place fire extinguishers next to doors that lead out of workshops. This way, if fire starts in the workshop, occupants will have to move in the direction of exits to get to fire extinguishers and not deeper into the building.

Putting together a home workshop can be fun and rewarding. Expect to change things around until you arrive at a floor plan that works best for the majority of your workshop endeavors. Have fun puttering, building, and fixing things, but always keep personal safety at the forefront of your thoughts for not only yourself but for everyone else who stops by for a visit or to help.

CHAPTER 1

Ideas for workshop designs

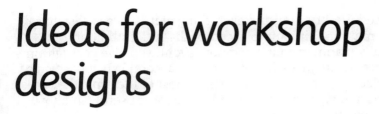

THERE IS NO magic formula for putting together first-class home workshops, nor is there an all-encompassing floor plan to fit everyone's needs and desires. Your home workshop must serve many functions:

- A place to fix household objects.

- Somewhere to make new things to decorate or improve your home's efficiency.

- A haven to escape the hustle and bustle of everyday life.

- A classroom where family members are taught how to safely use tools to repair or make things.

- A comfortable oasis where you and your's can putter, tinker, talk, learn, and have fun.

Study catalogs from Makita, Stanley, and Harbor Freight Tools to see what is available and how certain tools can serve different functions. Don't let your plans of an ideal workshop get carried away with thoughts about dozens of power tools, pieces of equipment, special accessories, optional attributes, elaborate systems, horns, bells, and whistles. With your workshop so crammed full of stuff, you won't have room to move! How will you get any work done? Keep things simple, comfortable, efficient, and, most important, safe.

Basic planning

Do-it-yourselfers dream of having separate workshops where their tools are permanently placed in convenient and organized locations ready for work at a moment's notice. They also drool over thoughts of spacious open areas where work is accomplished without obstructions. To accomplish those objectives, one must spend time planning.

Planning layout

A place for everything and everything in its place is easy to say, but sometimes difficult to accomplish—at least initially. By carefully planning your workshop layout, you give yourself time to contemplate just what you hope to accomplish, what types of projects you expect to undertake most of the time, the types of tools and equipment that will prove most useful, and how your projects will progress.

START WITH EXISTING SPACE— OR ADD SOME

If you're lucky enough to have a basement, garage or spare room, you have all the makings of a first class storage and work room.

But even without readily convertible space, there is a way to add the storage and work area you've always wanted: build on a storage room. Adequate storage can make a significant difference in the resale value of your home. And you just might be surprised at

how little it costs—particularly if you do some of the work yourself.

Once you have the basic structure, it's time to decide on the kind of storage units and built-ins you want to add. The best way to start is with the plans and ideas offered in this and other Western Wood Plan Sheets. The projects are easy to build, and all use standard, readily-available lumber.

For example, to make

the most efficient use of your usable space, you could build several of these storage modules side by side, as illustrated. By adding shelves, pegs and cupboards, you can accommodate almost anything you have to store, from games and groceries to garden equipment.

Also included are plans for a sturdy, easy-to-build workbench that's big enough to handle almost any size project. The plans

provide the basic structure—you lengthen or shorten it to fit the space you have available. Mobile bins, which are stored beneath the bench, take the strain out of handling heavy items.

Use these plans as the basic building blocks for your new storage area. For additional storage ideas, get a complete list of plans and publications from Western Wood Products Association. See back cover for details.

Designed by Czopek & Erdenberger, Interior Planning & Design, Portland, Oregon

Are you an avid woodworker who builds lots of big cabinet or furniture pieces? You'll need lots of open room. Do you prefer to spend time fixing small appliances and electronic gadgets? You'll need storage space for small parts and fasteners. Like to restore cars? You'll need a heavy-duty compressed-air system.

Many do-it-yourself magazines frequently carry articles about home workshops. Look through them for layout ideas. The Western Wood Products Association (WWPA) offers dozens of different plans for all sorts of home improvement projects. Many of the plans, such as the combination storage-and-workbench unit, are very inexpensive. Call or write the WWPA for a list of available plans.

Storage is always a concern around every workshop and the ideas in WWPA's Plan Sheet 50 might be perfect for you. With regard to storage units, take time to measure things you expect to put into them so that units can be built large enough. Measure height, length, and width of such things as 5-gallon buckets, scroll saws, bench-mounted sanders, small welders, and anything else you might want to store in a floor-level cabinet or an above-workbench cupboard.

Another excellent source of inexpensive plans for numerous home improvement projects is the American Plywood Association (APA). Any one of the handy work station plans they offer might be perfect for your workshop applications. APA plans generally cost around $2 and up. Call or write for a catalog list.

Is your workshop going to be cut out of a niche in the basement? Garage? Vacant bedroom? Will you be cramped for space and need to put everything away immediately after completing projects? Maybe you should consider a combination workbench and storage unit on wheels?

Toward the back of his deep two-car garage, Jim Yocum is constructing a 36-inch high, L-shaped cabinet with a 24-inch-wide work surface (see next page). In front of the cabinet is a 10-x-3-foot unit that will be equipped with heavy-duty locking wheels. In addition to mobility, the unit is the same height as Jim's table saw to ultimately serve as an out-feed table. This

arrangement provides an extension at the back of the saw onto which sheets of plywood will slide as they are pushed through and cut by the table saw.

Tool and supply storage is an important workshop concern. Will open shelves be subject to sawdust accumulation? Will enclosed cupboards with solid doors hamper your efforts to quickly find things? Maybe the combination of a few open shelves and some cabinets will best serve your needs.

Power tools and their accessories, intricate measuring devices, metalworking tools, and other objects subject to damage from

damp or dusty conditions are probably best stored in enclosed cabinets. For safety, especially when young children are around, consider power tool storage cabinets outfitted with lock-and-key mechanisms.

Some avid do-it-yourselfers completely finish workshop walls with pegboard. Pegboard placed at strategic locations around your workshop can prove most convenient for frequently used items such as squares, levels, wrenches, screwdrivers, etc.

If you decide to use pegboard, install ¼-inch pegboard for best results. It is heavier and stronger than thinner grades. Try out newly developed Sta-Put Color Pegs, too. Their patented design includes a special lug that snaps into pegboard holes directly below their hangers to keep pegs from falling off pegboard every time tools are retrieved. These pegs work great, hold up to 40 pounds, and are removable. You can put them in and pull them out anytime.

Structural concerns

Moisture is a workshop's enemy. It will cause improperly stacked wood to warp, tools to rust, and paint to peel. Moisture is especially bothersome for basements and unheated garages and outbuildings, so be sure the walls are covered with a vapor barrier to reduce dampness that could infiltrate workshop areas.

This basement wall is almost entirely below grade (next page, top). A major water problem has already been corrected through a series of foundation drains. However, further efforts are underway to prevent future moisture saturation. The wall was first covered with 4-mil plastic and then taped in place. A new 2-x-4 wall was built against the plastic and nailed to the floor joists above and secured to the concrete floor below with anchor bolts. Once electrical wiring is installed, the new wall will be filled with Owens-Corning faced insulation. Facing serves as an additional vapor barrier.

How much electricity will your shop need? Will you be doing a lot of welding or working with large pieces of equipment? Has your workshop been added to the main house or is it a separate building? These are questions that must be addressed in the planning stages. The more tools, lights, and equipment you expect to operate, the more electricity you'll need.

Certified electrician (and son-in-law) Steve Brown is busy dismantling our disconnected main electrical service panel and subpanel (below it). A new 200-amp service panel with a 40-breaker service is scheduled to replace it. NOTE: Only certified electricians should ever be allowed to attempt any type of a main electrical service panel alteration.

Before a decision was made to go with a 200-amp service, a representative from the power company was asked to look at the existing service to determine if it was sufficient to supply a larger panel. Once base electrical service was identified, Steve calculated how much power our new shop would need, how much the existing home required, and then decided that—

Electrical needs

Doors & windows

because the hot water, furnace, and clothes dryer were served by natural gas—a 200-amp service would work just fine.

More information about electrical supplies is covered in chapter 5. Plan to consult with a power company representative and an electrician before starting on workshop finishing tasks.

Home garages are notorious for being cluttered with plumbing pipes, hot water tanks, and other utility features. One way to hide some items is with framed door units. This is a main water supply shut-off valve found inside its own little enclosure. You might consider similar accessories for sewer clean-outs and crawl space entries.

Workshops do not have to look like typical workshops. They can be neat, clean, and tidy home additions. Along with finished drywall, paint, and trim, an attractive Stanley steel entry door offers solid workshop security and eye appeal.

Windows are another important consideration. If security is not a problem around your workshop, consider the addition of windows or skylights. Although many avid do-it-yourselfers prefer to keep their tools and equipment out of sight in windowless workshops, you must determine whether or not security is a problem, and if windows would compliment your workshop and its environment.

We chose to install Eagle wood windows in both our workshop and second-level living area. Because windows are permanent installations, you must carefully weigh the advantages of long-lasting and energy-efficient windows against economy models that might not last as long and will not offer the same level of energy efficiency.

Likewise, you need to determine which window style—casement, awning, double-hung, and so on—offers you the best service. We opted for casements because they allow for the greatest amount of air flow into and out of living and workshop areas. Our windows came complete with screens (even for the workshop). Screens are excellent features in summertime when you want plenty of air flow without bees, hornets, flies, mosquitoes, and other pesky insects along with it.

Finishing touches

How many home workshops have you seen that were virtually unfinished with bare stud walls, dirt floors, open ceiling-to-attic areas, and the like? John Gittings built a beautiful 40-x-50-foot workshop with a 20-foot ceiling and two large bay doors. He is a do-it-yourselfer with interests in woodworking, construction, metalworking, and automotive projects. However, John has been living with a major workshop mistake for many years; he moved into the shop before it was finished. It still has a dirt floor.

Don't make a similar mistake. Plan your workshop so that you have all of the basics installed before designing and building workbenches, cabinets, cupboards, shelves, and then filling them with stuff. Likewise, once you reach a point where you build and install workshop attributes, don't forget to finish them. Make time to coat bare wood with a sealer, stain, or paint.

To keep sawdust from accumulating under drywall and cabinets edges, consider the installation of cove molding, which is attractive, efficient, and easy to install.

Serious planning, conscientious attention to detail, and patience will result in a home workshop that looks great, functions efficiently, and rewards you with comfort and convenience.

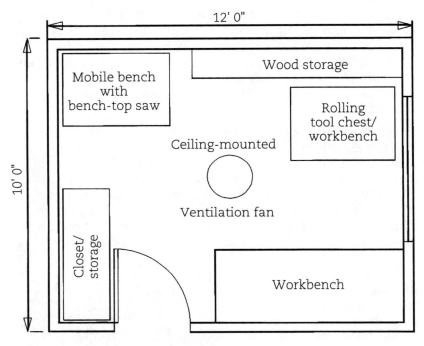

Room conversion

Floor plans

Designing a workshop floor plan to satisfy the needs of someone else would be like trying to handpick a boyfriend for your teenage daughter; they ain't gonna like it! Everybody has different tastes, likes, and dislikes. Your workshop is essentially an extension of you—your hobbies, craft interests, home repair notions, ambitions, and choice in creature comforts. So design it to fit you like you would a cozy easy chair or a pair of favorite shoes.

It might help to understand that service areas are often set up in triangular patterns so that workers or users can locate their three main areas of interest within a triangular pattern. Kitchens are set up that way: the refrigerator at one point of the triangle, stove and cook-top at another, and food preparation area (sink and counter) at the third. Think of your shop in a similar fashion. Place the wood or the supply storage at one point, the most frequently used piece of equipment (like a table saw) at another point, and the workbench at the third. Design your shop with easy and unobstructed access to the most frequently used accessories and then adjust as necessary.

A vacant room

A vacant bedroom might serve as a perfect retreat for a hobbyist, just be aware that sawdust and other pollutants could infiltrate into heat ducts and under doors to contaminate other parts of your home. A ventilation or dust-collection system might be an appropriate investment.

A basement

Basements make fine workshops for many homeowners. One of the more common problems associated with this arrangement is access and egress. It might be easy enough to build a small sailboat down there, but how do you get it out? You'll also have to make concessions for sawdust and other airborne pollutants, and you will have to forget about any spray painting or other

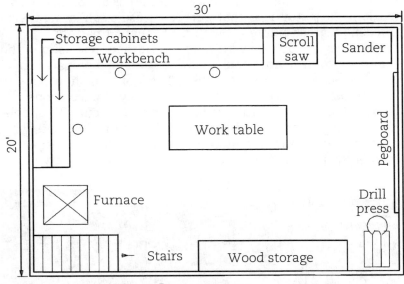

Basement area

activity that involves flammable materials. A furnace pilot light or flame could ignite flammable vapors to cause a fire or explosion. Ventilation is a concern in any workshop but especially in basements that don't have windows.

A one-car garage

With a bit of practical ingenuity, you can devise a viable workshop at the front of a one-car garage. Take advantage of upper spaces along side walls for storage cabinets. Build a workbench at the front, or at least construct a heavy table top hinged to the wall and outfitted with fold-out legs so there is room for a car inside. Mount bigger tools, such as a table saw, a lathe, a shaper, or a jointer on heavy-duty locking casters so they can be rolled back to a storage space when jobs are completed.

A two-car garage

Jim Yocum has put together a nice workshop in his 24-x-34-foot, two-car garage. You can do the same with some careful planning. Mount bigger pieces of equipment on top of sturdy workbenches outfitted with heavy-duty locking casters so the benches can be rolled out for work and then easily put away.

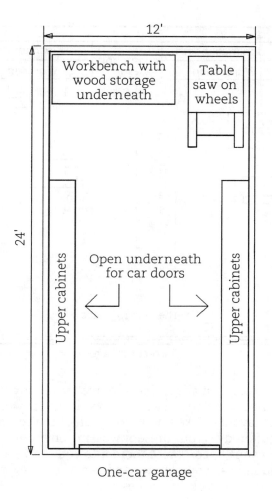

12'

Workbench with wood storage underneath

Table saw on wheels

24'

Upper cabinets

Open underneath for car doors

Upper cabinets

One-car garage

For a bona fide, dedicated, and separate workshop facility, take plenty of time to contemplate your overall work and comfort needs. Bathroom facilities, refrigerators, sound systems, and telephones make great workshop amenities. Planning should include all underground utilities such as plumbing, electric, natural gas, and telephone lines. Before you cover walls, be certain you have addressed your utility needs, as well as those for compressed-air piping, intercom speaker wire, ventilation ducts and fans, etc.

An outbuilding

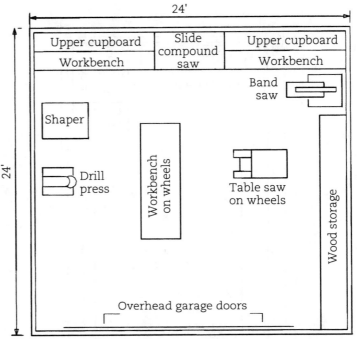

Upper cupboard	Slide compound saw	Upper cupboard
Workbench		Workbench

Band saw

Shaper

Workbench on wheels

Drill press

Table saw on wheels

Wood storage

Overhead garage doors

Two-car garage

If you have been an active do-it-yourselfer for any length of time, chances are you have some good ideas for workshop floor plans and layouts. Take into account all of the comfortable features offered by your present working environment and, at least for a start, incorporate them into your new shop. Then grow gradually as you plan for and can afford new tools, equipment, and workshop accessories.

For those with limited exposure to the do-it-yourself world, plan for your workshop design by reading various home-improvement and woodworking magazines. Start small in a garage or basement with just a few essential hand tools, a power drill, a circular saw, a jigsaw, and maybe a table saw. Determine what type of home improvement endeavors you like the most: cabinet building, furniture restoring, built-in convenience installations, room remodeling or updating, interior decorating, and so on. Once your do-it-yourself passions are known, you'll have a much better idea of the type of workshop arrangement that will best suit your overall needs.

Windows & doors

WORKSHOP PLANS should take windows and doors into account. The number, size, and type of windows are primary considerations. Is theft and burglary a problem around your workshop? Would you prefer to maximize security by eliminating windows? Would you like to enjoy plenty of open window ventilation and lots of bright sunlight?

Every workshop must have a door. Remodeled bedroom and basement workshops will already have one entrance. Larger workshops should be outfitted with doors to accommodate the materials and objects that go into and out of the structure. For avid woodworkers and home-improvement do-it-yourselfers, double-entry doors, offering open widths of from 5 to 6 feet, might be just right. For automotive and boat projects, workshops need big-bay (garage) doors.

Extra large workshops with tall ceilings should have 10-foot or higher doors to allow plenty of room for motor homes, boats, and other substantial vehicles to pass through. Look ahead to the type of work you expect to undertake in your workshop and then plan door sizes accordingly.

Windows

Natural sunlight brings out true colors in everything. While no type of artificial light can take sunlight's place, fluorescent, halogen, and incandescent fixtures in appropriate numbers will certainly light up workshops to more than adequate requirements. Many professional craftspeople and avid do-it-yourselfers prefer the addition of natural sunlight into their workshops. Sunlight helps you to clearly perceive the effects of stain and paint on projects. Others relish sunlight for aesthetic reasons. Most people appreciate cool breezes through open windows on warm summer days.

Windows are available in many different sizes, shapes, and styles. These are Eagle wood-awning windows. They open from the bottom and tilt out. Notice how the wood-frame corners are

made with one end going past the other. This design makes these windows extra strong and secure. Two panes of glass separated by an air space filled with argon helps to make them very energy efficient. In addition, Low E glass, helps to keep heat inside during cold weather and heat out during hot weather. The principle of Low E is similar to a Thermos jug that keeps cold drinks cold and hot drinks hot.

Many types and sizes of windows are available. Talk with a professional before making final decisions. Because windows are rather permanent installations, it would be wise to install top-quality models now rather than replace inexpensive units later.

Wearing safety goggles and with all hand and wrist jewelry removed, Keith Rieber uses a Makita Cordless Recipro Saw to trim away excess exterior wall sheathing in preparation for a window installation. Window sizes must be calculated before the walls are constructed so that rough openings can be properly framed.

Rough openings

Rough-opening window sizes are available through your window representative. Most rough openings are from ½ inch to 1 inch wider and taller than the actual window sizes. Note, however, that some manufacturers calculate rough openings differently. Also keep in mind that oversized rough openings must be filled in to offer proper window support and windows simply won't fit into openings that are too small.

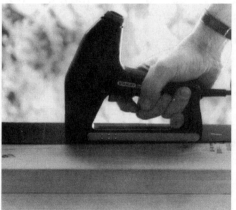

Once you have determined that the windows fit inside the rough openings, line exterior openings with 15-pound building paper. Staple the paper in place. Techniques for lining window openings with products such as DuPont's Tyvek Housewrap insulation are explained in subsequent paragraphs.

Shims

Windows are shimmed to ensure perfect and level fits. Because their frames are so sturdy, some windows need only small shims at the corners. Other window styles require shims in the middle as well as at the corners. With his safety goggles in place, Luke uses a couple of 8d nails to secure this window shim in a corner.

At least two people are needed to lift and set windows into openings. This is done from the outside. One person holds the window secure by lightly pushing on it from the outside. The other person uses a tape measure to ensure that the window is evenly centered in its opening, and employs a level to see that the window rests perfectly flat on its bottom sill. Once the window is positioned properly, 8d galvanized nails are used to secure the nailing fins to the building.

Adding a window

There might be times when you want to install a window that was not accounted for in original building plans, or you might want to add a window to an existing workshop. To do this, first determine where the window will go. Next, carefully cut away interior drywall and frame openings from the inside. NOTE: Holes made on interior walls will have to be bigger than the windows to allow adequate room for wood-framing work.

Be certain there are no obstructions on the exterior of your building at the location of your new window. Assured that your window placement is correct, use a drill to bore holes at each

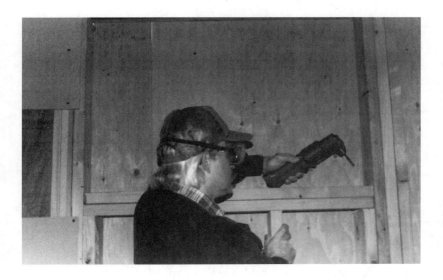

corner of your new window's rough opening. This is done from the inside as a means of accurately determining where to cut the opening from the outside.

Use a long level as a guide to make straight pencil lines to outline the window opening. The holes bored from the inside of the wall will designate rough-opening corners. When cutting through existing siding and older sheathing, be on the alert for nails. Try scraping away exterior wall paint from underneath your pencil lines. Pull all nails located near lines to ensure that the saw blades will not run into them. Afterward, make fresh pencil lines to show where window openings must be cut.

Next, cut out the window opening. We used a Makita circular saw adjusted to cut just ½ inch deep (the thickness of the sheathing). With the front part of the saw's shoe held firmly against sheathing and positioned so the blade was directly above a line, the saw guard was held partially open with one hand while the saw was slowly pushed down and moved forward with the other hand.

Once the blade had completely cut through a small section of sheathing, the guard was released and cutting continued. We used the reciprocal saw to clean up corner cuts because circular saw blades cannot make complete cuts at corners unless the blade is allowed to cut past corners on top surfaces.

When using a circular saw to make an initial cut into wood, always pay strict attention to what you are doing. Be ready to release the saw's trigger and stop the action anytime a saw bogs down or fails to move smoothly.

With the rough window opening successfully cut out, we secured Tyvek Housewrap to every other stud at the top, middle, and bottom, as well as around window and door openings. NOTE: It is easiest to install Tyvek Housewrap with at least two people; more workers will come in handy for second-story operations.

Once the Tyvek has been wrapped and secured, go back to rough window openings and use a sharp utility knife to cut from corner to corner. Fold flaps around window openings toward the inside and secure with staples.

On occasion, you might need to wrap your new workshop structure with Tyvek after windows have already been installed. In this case, carefully cut the Tyvek close to and around window frames and then seal free edges with contractor's tape. This red-colored tape can be found at lumberyards and home-improvement centers.

Contractor's tape should also be used to secure all seams and cuts made in the material, such as those needed to accommodate water spigots and exterior light fixtures.

Always test fit your window after installing shims. Use a level to ensure that each unit rests perfectly flat on sills. As necessary, install thinner or thicker shims in order to level units properly. Notice that this window rests perfectly level on the first test fit. This is because time was taken to carefully install the 2-x-6 bottom sill flat and level.

The window was removed after a test fit and the exterior window-edge opening is now being prepared with a bead of DAP sealant. Sealant helps to prevent air and moisture from seeping in through exterior siding and under nailing fins. It also helps to keep warm air indoors.

Once a solid bead of sealant is placed around the entire window perimeter, the window is placed into position. Again, measurements must be taken on the inside to ensure that the window is evenly centered before nails are driven through the nailing fins and into the window framework.

Nails are driven through holes in the nailing fins along both sides and the bottom. Nail heads are driven down completely until they firmly hold the nailing fins tightly against the window frame. At the top, nails are started above the nailing fin and then bent down. Top nailing fins must be secured in this manner (with bent nails) to prevent them from being solidly affixed to headers.

Over time, large headers tend to slightly bow down as a result of the weight they must support. Should top window edges be firmly secured to them, pressure from bowed headers would be transferred onto the tops of windows. This could cause window frames to bow. Eventually, you might find problems getting windows to open and cracks might develop in the glass.

Doors

Large garage doors are heavy, and they often require tightly coiled spring mechanisms for their operation. For the most part, plan to have experienced professionals install large bay or garage doors. They have access to special tools and equipment.

Regular doors, even double-entry models, are relatively simple to install. Much like windows, you must prepare door rough openings according to the manufacturer's specifications.

Our 5-foot-wide Eagle French door came from the factory requiring only nailing fins to be screwed in place around the exterior sides and top. As with windows, openings must be correctly sized with sill's level. (Shown at bottom left.)

A ½-inch piece of plywood was installed on top of the subfloor to serve as a base for the door. This was done because ½-inch particleboard will be installed later over the existing ¾-inch subfloor. A few beads of DAP sealant have been placed on the sill in preparation for the door's installation.

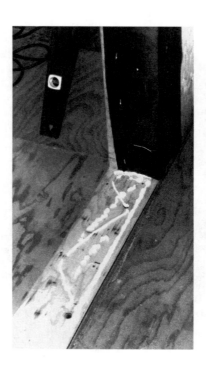

We used starter-course cedar shingles as shims for the sides of this door. However, any wood material can be used for shims. Shims are placed at each hinge location as a means to square the door in its opening. (Shown at bottom right of page 22.)

Janna uses a 4-foot Stanley level to check the door's plumb position. Notice that this unit's wood bracing is still in place, as seen through the glass, according to instructions. Once we determined that the door was properly positioned, nails were used to secure the unit in its rough opening. Nails were bent over the top nailing fin, the same as for windows.

Along with secured nailing fins, doors must also be supported with long screws that go through the hinges and all the way into adjacent rough-opening studs.

These hinges feature four openings into which screws are mounted. Two of the screws hold the door to its frame, while two others are saved for extra-long screws that are driven into rough-opening studs at installation. Instructions for most doors and windows are quite specific. It helps to study the instructions before you actually start work.

Once our French door was firmly secured to the rough opening, we installed the handles and hardware. Refer to the installation instructions to ensure that components are assembled correctly and in the right sequence.

Once handles and hardware have been put on most doors, installation operations are generally complete. Our unit proved to be an exception because Eagle French doors have additional adjustment mechanisms built into their hinges. Check the instructions supplied by the manufacturer of your door.

Weatherstripping helps to prevent air, dirt, and water from seeping indoors. After your wood door has been sealed and stained, place a small dab of silicone lubricant on your finger and rub it onto the rubber weatherstrip to help it glide easily across the sill. NOTE: Silicone lubricants greatly hinder stain or paint applications by causing the stain or paint to "bubble" or "fisheye." Apply lubricant after stain or paint has cured.

This 36-inch-wide Stanley steel entry door is about the smallest size suitable for a workshop. Once rough openings are lined with building paper or Tyvek Housewrap, tilt the door into place and begin shimming and leveling.

Shims are placed at hinges and pushed in or pulled out until the door frame is plumb. Shims should be tapered like wedges. Once the door is properly positioned, long screws are installed through hinge-plate openings and into the rough-opening stud.

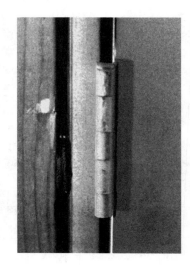

As with the French door, this steel entry model has two screws in place on each hinge to support the door in its frame. Each hinge had two remaining openings for the insertion of long screws.

Door finish work

Door trim is secured with finishing nails. Use a nail set to drive the nails partially into the wood to make room for wood putty. Fill holes with putty and, when dry, use 240 or finer sandpaper to smooth the surface in preparation for stain or paint.

Door hardware is not difficult to install. Complete packages come with instructions and templates. We used one from Weiser Lock. Templates are taped to doors to designate exactly where holes need to be bored for latches, throws, and deadbolts. Some doors like the Eagle and Stanley models described in this chapter have predrilled handle and lock holes.

Because door jamb plates vary in size and shape from company to company, few predrilled doors are notched for plates. You will have to make notches with a sharp chisel.

Simply insert latch-throw components into openings and trace plate edges onto jambs with a soft pencil. Remove throws and tap your chisel edge along pencil lines to create a border. With your chisel's beveled edge facing down, lightly tap it with a mallet to gently peel wood strips from the door jambs.

Installation instructions offer handy tips on how to designate plate locations for door-frame jambs. Follow instructions closely and chisel lightly; take out only small slices of wood with each pass. Test fit plates often to guard against going too deep. Have patience and work slowly.

Irregularities along the edges of door jamb plates are easily filled with wood putty and then sanded before painting. Door handles and locks are commonly installed first, then removed for staining or painting. This allows installers to repair minor scratches or imperfections with wood putty and sandpaper on bare sealed wood before finishing.

Once you have installed all window, door, and exterior-siding, you can stain or paint the outside of your new workshop. To make painting a lot easier and faster, consider using an airless paint machine. The HousePainter, made by Campbell Hausfeld, draws paint or stain right from the can. Materials are forced through the hose and spray gun at high pressure. Be sure to read, understand, and follow all operating and safety instructions.

Skylights & attic ventilation

FOR INCREASED illumination, consider adding skylights or roof windows to your workshop. Skylights are often made with acrylic or plastic and roof windows are constructed with glass. Ventilating roof windows and some types of skylights can be opened to relieve stuffy workshops.

Attic ventilators are large fans that pull hot or moist air outdoors through a roof opening. In hot weather, attic ventilators help to cool buildings by circulating air. In moist climates, they reduce moisture accumulation.

Skylights & roof windows

Skylight and roof-window openings can usually be positioned between roof trusses or rafters. Some brands require a solid 2-x-4 frame that rests on top of the roof structure. Units are placed on top of 2 × 4s. These Leslie-Locke roof windows are supported by L-shaped brackets that are secured to their hardwood frame on one side and roofs on the other.

The large piece of metal you see at the top of this unit is *flashing*. Pieces of flashing are placed against roof windows and then sandwiched between the courses of roof shingles to prevent rainwater from seeping inside. Follow the manufacturer's instructions to open the window. Have at least one other person on hand to help with any skylight or roof-window projects.

Place the free window on top of a piece of cardboard to prevent scratching the glass. Double-pane and argon-filled units are heavy, so have a helper assist you.

Install L-brackets or other hardware according to the manufacturer's instructions. If your roof is sheathed with plywood, simply attach the L-brackets according to given dimensions. If your roof is skip-sheathed with 1× boards or planking, you should confirm that the instruction's L-bracket dimensions will result in brackets secured on top of a piece of skip-sheathing and not in a gap located between two boards.

Be certain that all L-brackets are positioned an equal distance from bottom wood frame edges. This will ensure that the roof window sits flat on the roof surface and not at an angle.

Have a helper assist you by holding the roof window steady while you secure the L-brackets with the screws provided. A cordless drill makes this task easy. When using a power drill to install L-bracket screws, be sure its torque adjustment is set on low as you start out. Driving screws in too hard could cause the roof window's hardwood frame to split or crack. Once all four L-brackets have been positioned, the unit is ready for installation.

You can quickly determine where skylights or roof windows should be installed on unfinished workshops, but for an existing workshop with an established roof, you should first decide where units should be placed at the ceiling level. Drive a nail through that spot and then locate its protruding tip in the attic. Look around to be sure there are no obstructions that would block a skylight or roof-window installation.

Positioning the skylight

Determine the exact location for your skylight or roof window. After you have confirmed there are no obstructions on the roof,

designate the outline of your skylight or roof window by driving four nails through the roof from inside the attic. Each nail will represent a corner of the skylight or roof window corner.

Locate the four nails on the roof. Remove shingles from inside the square or rectangle shape outlined by the nails. Once you reach roofing paper, use a steel square and utility knife to carefully cut that material away from your outline.

Installing the skylight

Use a saw to cut away sheathing. CAUTION: Do not cut through nails! The nails immediately will dull your saw blade and could cause injury if chunks of nails or saw blades are broken off and sent flying.

If the installation requires the removal of a small piece of rafter, blocks will have to be installed at the top and bottom to support rafter ends that have been cut.

It is easiest to install skylights and roof windows that fit between existing roof rafters. However, there are times when interior walls, plumbing vent pipes, and other obstacles mandate units be located in specific spots. Such installations frequently require the rafters to be cut and blocked.

Cutting and blocking rafters is awkward work. In addition, prefabricated roof trusses are not designed to be cut arbitrarily. Building inspectors and truss manufacturers highly recommend (if not require) that truss engineers design specific sets of blocking plans for trusses that need to be cut for any reason. If at all possible, plan to install skylights or roof windows between trusses.

Rafters are different and, as long as they are blocked with material of equal size, there is generally no problem. Use a plumb bob and tape measure to accurately determine where to cut rafters. Don't forget to account for skylight or roof-window frames. A few marks, notes, and lines were made before we actually arrived at an accurate cutting mark.

New roofs simply sheathed do not carry a great deal of weight. Most of the time, you can cut rafters and then block as needed for the roof window. However, existing roofs support a great deal of weight. For those, block first before cutting rafters.

Secure sheathing ends to rafter blocking as necessary. With all the rafter work complete, get someone to help you lift the skylight or roof window to the roof surface and prepare for its installation.

The L-bracket on this roof window was positioned an inch or so off the instruction guidelines to ensure that it would rest on top of a skip-sheathing board and not a gap. Before securing units to the roof with screws, have someone go underneath to help position them squarely inside openings.

Weatherproofing the skylight

Once the unit is secured to the roof, work begins with flashing, roofing paper, and shingles. This crucial stage of the installation determines whether or not your skylight or roof window unit will leak during rain or snow showers.

Our Leslie-Locke roof windows feature a rubber boot around unit tops. Metal flashing is placed under boot lips to create weather-tight seals. The units we installed require no sealer or caulking.

Flashing operations start at the bottom and work up toward roof peaks just like ordinary roofing tasks. Flashing first goes in at the very bottom of the skylight or roof window unit, with subsequent side flashing and then tops.

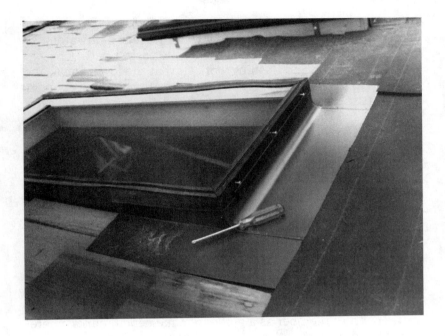

For our cedar-shake roof, we placed a piece of flashing down on top of the roofing paper, which partially extended over the top of a shake. Then, we put a shake over it and secured it to the roof with staples from a pneumatic staple gun. We were careful to avoid putting staples into the flashing.

The next piece of flashing was positioned on top of that shake and extended down far enough to cover a portion of the previous piece of flashing.

Flashing installations for asphalt-fiberglass shingled roofs are a bit different. Read installation instructions for definitive flashing instructions.

Because our roof was covered with thick-butt cedar shakes, some flashing pieces had to be trimmed in order to make them fit properly. Tasks that involve metal cutting require careful attention to detail. Because metal edges will be very sharp, wear leather gloves.

While engaged in skylight or roof-window flashing work, understand and keep in mind how water travels. Rainwater always seeks its lowest level by way of the easiest path. Jobs related to roofing and flashing work start at the lowest level and work up in such a way as to block water pathways at every point and, in turn, cause the rainwater to run down and off the eaves.

After you have successfully installed your skylights or roof windows, box in their light wells. For the most part, you simply need to erect a 2 × 4 frame to support pieces of drywall. The 2 × 4s are cut to fit between rafters and trusses to offer support for drywall nailed or screwed to them.

Drywall must be supported at all corners and in the middle for pieces wider than 16 inches. Because you will be working with angles, take your time during this operation.

Bring the 2 × 4's into the attic and hold them next to existing rafter or truss members in the position desired. Use an existing rafter or truss member as a guide to make pencil marks where 2 × 4s need to be cut. A pneumatic nailing gun comes in real handy to secure these cut boards.

Patience and a lot of measuring will be rewarded with drywall pieces that fit on the first try. Use drywall mud and tape to finish light wells. Seal bare drywall with a quality conditioner as recommended on paint label instructions. Paint light wells any desired color or trim with wood strips.

Attic ventilation

During hot summer months, workshop attics can become virtual ovens. Much of the heat trapped in attics will radiate into active workshop areas.

Likewise, damp weather can cause unusual amounts of moisture to become trapped in attic spaces. Excess moisture and humidity can cause problems with mildew and dry rot. Extreme cases could result in water droplets falling off interior roof surfaces, eventually leaking onto workshop ceilings, inside walls, and almost anywhere else.

Minimal attic ventilation soffit and roof vents are greatly enhanced with the addition of an attic ventilator. Equipped with its own thermostat, this Leslie-Locke unit turns on and off automatically to help keep attics properly ventilated. In addition, this unit can be equipped with an optional humidistat that will cause the unit to operate during high-humidity conditions.

Installation instructions for this unit were quite simple and very similar to those for skylights and roof windows. A template was printed on the unit's carton to designate the correct size hole to cut in the roof surface.

Use a cordless reciprocal saw, jig saw, or hole saw to cut a round hole in the roof. Remember that you will have to run electrical power to the unit before it can operate. It might be easiest to install and then test the electrical wiring tasks before buttoning up the roof work.

As with skylights and roof windows, roofing paper and shingles are brought up to the base of the unit first. The rectangular box extending out the side of this attic ventilator is where the unit's electrical wires are connected to electric supply wiring.

Because roof ventilators are already outfitted with their own flashing, place the unit on top of the lower shingle roll with its top portion tucked under a piece of roofing paper. Roofing paper and wood shingle work continued up the sides and across the top to create a weather-tight seal.

Interior workshop ventilation

Unless you expect to create an unusually large amount of sawdust or other atmospheric pollution in your workshop, windows, ventilating roof windows, and doors should offer you plenty of ventilation. If power equipment is equipped with dust collectors, you will have even better working conditions.

Should your workshop require additional ventilation, look into prefabricated systems designed for workshops. Safety and supply stores and commercial heating and air-conditioning companies should be able to help you design a system using regular heat-ducting materials.

Ducting

Heat registers are available in many different styles and models. They can be made to serve as air ducts to pull sawdust or air sprays away from concentrated areas and out through ducting to the outdoors. Home centers generally carry a wide variety of ducting connections that enable users to custom design and fit specific installations.

Duct work for workshop ventilation systems is set up like regular heating systems. The difference is when you hook up the ventilation system to the intake side of your workshop fan so that it will draw air through and then outside instead of like heater fans that bring cool air into a furnace and then force hot air out.

In essence, a workshop ventilation system is simply a series of wide ducts that run to specific locations as a means to pull in large amounts of air that have been polluted with sawdust, sprays, or other airborne debris. Drawn in by a high-CFM (cubic-feet-per-minute) fan, ducting should continue off the discharge side of the fan to the outdoors.

If you plan to spray paint much in your workshop—which will result in a highly polluted atmosphere of flammable vapors— you must confer with a professional heating and air-conditioning contractor. Fans for use in these conditions must be explosion proof. They are specially made in such a way that electrical arcs or sparks from their motors and windings are totally encapsulated to avoid any potential for creating a possible fire hazard.

Plumbing

SIMPLE PLUMBING consists of getting fresh water into certain areas and sending waste products out of certain areas. Fresh water is brought in under pressure through a series of copper pipes soldered together. Waste products flow out under the force of gravity through large-diameter plastic drainpipes glued together.

Sinks with hot and cold running water make excellent workshop attributes. Along with normal use for cleaning hands and various tools or materials, a source of fresh water can be considered a safety option. Use fresh water to flush eyes or other body parts in cases of contamination by debris or strong chemicals.

Household and workshop drain systems rely upon a series of pipes that lead from sinks, showers, bathtubs, and toilets to a main sewer pipe. The main sewer pipe is connected to a municipal sewer line or septic system. All of these pipes must be positioned at a downward angle so that gravity can pull waste products out and away from structures and into sewer or septic systems. Sole exceptions are structures located below the sewer line or septic system levels, such as basements, that require pumps to force waste up to main sewer lines.

Your first impression of all the different plumbing and pipe fittings should not be one of confusion. Envision the pieces as handy helpers designed to make your plumbing jobs easier. Elbows, tees, wyes, and other parts allow you to route drains around corners, down walls, and wherever they need to go.

The large pipe in the middle is a main stack. It runs down to the main sewer line. All second-level drains will empty into it. The pipe on the left is a drain for an upstairs shower. The pipe on the right is a vent pipe for the workshop shower. All drainpipes must be vented to fresh air, usually through pipes that stick through the roof. Vents prevent drains from creating vacuums as water rushes downhill.

Drain system

A 4-inch, inside-diameter main sewer line runs under our workshop. Connections for a main stack and the workshop floor-level toilet and shower were made to it before the concrete floor was poured. Here, a 3-inch, inside-diameter reducer is attached as the first leg of the main stack to the workshop's sinks and second-level bathroom facilities.

Connecting plastic ABS drainpipe is easy. Clean and roughen pipe and fitting edges with sandpaper, spread ABS-rated glue with a cap-mounted brush, and put parts together. The tee on the floor to the left will be attached upright to the stack with the small inlet positioned toward the left to serve as a connection for the workshop's bathroom sink. A basic rule of thumb for drainpipe sizes is:

4-inch, side-diameter pipe	main sewer lines
3-inch, inside-diameter pipe	main stacks and all toilets
2-inch inside-diameter pipe	showers and bathtubs
1½-inch, inside-diameter pipe	sinks and vanities

Because main stack 3-inch pipe is too large to fit inside 2-x-4 walls, you will have to build 2-x-6 walls. On the other hand, 2-x-4 walls are fine for 2-inch and 1½-inch pipe. Just to the left of the main stack and in that stack's 2-x-6 wall, preparations are being made to run a 1½-inch drain line for the workshop bathroom sink. Each vertical mark on successive 2-x-6 studs is about a half inch higher than the one before it to ensure that waste water runs down toward the stack and sewer line.

Hole saws work great for drilling holes in studs for drainpipe. A Makita Plumbers and Electricians Kit offers hole-saw sizes to accommodate most needs. Drilling holes in studs is easier with a ½-inch angle drill.

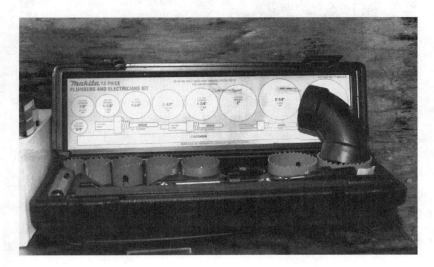

To prevent wood plugs from lodging inside hole saws once holes are bored, drill in from one stud side until the pilot drill goes through the other side. Then, complete the boring task from that other side. A large portion of the bored section will stick out from the hole saw for easy retrieval.

To get a long section of drainpipe to fit through wall studs, holes were drilled from the stack all the way out to the end of the wall. Pipe was inserted from the end of the wall to the tee at the main stack. Pipe runs downhill from left to right toward the stack.

Drain stubs that stick out from wall finishes to which sink drains are attached generally sit about 12 inches off the floor. Once the long section of drainpipe was installed and glued to the tee at the stack, it was cut at the point where a workshop bathroom sink is planned. A 1½-inch tee was attached to the end of the drainpipe, with an inlet pointing straight up and horizontally level. A short section of pipe will be glued to it with another tee attached to it that will have its inlet facing out toward the sink. Another section of pipe will be attached to the top of that tee and run straight up toward the roof where it will be connected to the main stack as a vent.

This pipe exits the stack's 2-x-6 wall, makes a 90-degree turn, and goes into a 2-x-4 wall that separates the workshop from an office area. We cut a section from a 2-x-4 stud in order to get an elbow to fit. Simpson Strong-Tie nailing plates cover openings in the stud. Nailing plates protect pipe from drywall nails or screws. Nailing plates are required for all pipes and electrical wires located closer than 1½ inches to stud nailing surfaces.

Ground-level workshop drain systems consist of pipes that run from sinks to main stacks and pipes that run from sinks up to venting locations. Vent pipes can run separately up to and through roofs or run back through attic areas to upper stack sections for venting. The advantage of running vent pipes back to stacks is to minimize the number of vent pipes that stick out of roofs.

A workshop located on a second-floor level or new living areas constructed on top of a workshop building might also require some plumbing work. Second-level drainpipes must consistently run downhill toward main drain stacks. This will entail drilling or cutting holes in floor joists.

I-beam style truss joists are delivered with specific sets of instructions regarding the number, size, and spacing of all holes that can be cut out of the units' webbing. At no time can the solid wood top or bottom runners be cut or notched. Your local building department has information regarding the same specifications for cutting or drilling holes in solid lumber (2 × 10s, 2 × 12s, and the like). Rules governing the placement of holes in floor joists will vary from region to region.

Access for drainpipe through the floor joists to accommodate an upstairs bathroom is accomplished by cutting a hole through an exterior wall's 2-x-10 block and then through all floor joists in a straight line.

A long section of 2-inch drainpipe was inserted from outdoors through the 2-x-10 block and fed through to join up with existing drainpipe at the top right. The hole in the 2-x-10 block will also provide access for freshwater copper pipe. Once plumbing work is done, the piece of wood cut out of the 2-x-10 block will be put back with wood glue and caulking.

Notice the reducing wye at the lower section of this 3-inch stack. Both ends of the wye are 3 inches, and the wye section is 2 inches. This 2-inch drain line has a tee attached just above the wall's top plate. The inlet on the tee will serve a second-level shower drain. The 2-inch line continues up the wall and through the second floor where it will be routed to the main stack for venting. Note that nailing plates are in position to protect the pipes from being damaged by drywall nails or screws or other fasteners that might be inserted into the wall later.

Fresh water must be pumped into structures. Municipal water systems include strategically located pump stations that pump water from lakes and rivers to reservoirs, and eventually to structures. Private wells incorporate separate pumps that force water from wells to pressurized storage tanks. Water is then routed from storage tanks to faucets, toilets, and so on. Whereas gravity controls waste water flow from sinks and bathroom facilities, pressure from pumps forces fresh water to flow out of faucets and other outlets. Because fresh water is always kept under pressure, copper pipes can be routed in any direction.

Freshwater plumbing

Copper water pipes and fittings are soldered together to run from a main service line to all points within a structure. Here, three ½-inch copper cold water lines run off a ¾-inch distribution line. Generally, a 1-inch, inside-diameter main water line is routed from a municipal system's water main at the street and into structures.

Copper pipes are routed through structures by use of various fittings. Fittings are attached to pipes through a sweating process. Pipe ends and fitting inlets are cleaned and scoured with emery cloth, covered with flux (a waxy material), pushed

Copper pipes & fittings

together, and then heated up with a propane torch. Once fittings and pipe ends have been heated up to a certain temperature, solder is placed against connections where it instantly melts and is sucked into fittings.

Molten solder dripping off copper connections is a sign that fittings have been completely filled. At that point, carefully wipe a water-soaked rag over connections to clean away excess solder.

Sweating copper pipes and fittings together is very easy. To master the technique, purchase a section of pipe and a few fittings for practice. After cleaning, sanding, and applying flux to both a pipe end and the inlet of the fitting to be sweated on, aim the torch flame at the end of the fitting. Do not aim the flame at the pipe. Continue to heat the fitting with the torch in one hand and a roll of solder in the other.

Once flux starts boiling around the fitting inlet edge, touch the tip of an uncoiled section of solder to the fitting. If the solder does not immediately start to melt, back off and continue heating the fitting. Wait a few moments and then touch the solder to the fitting again. When fittings have been heated to a proper temperature, solder will melt instantly and be immediately drawn into the fitting. The process only takes a minute or so. As excess solder begins to drip, turn off the torch and wipe the fitting with a soaking wet rag.

Your workshop will need to be served by two freshwater pipes; one for cold water and another for hot. A tee is installed on the main 1-inch, freshwater service line. Cold water from the main goes straight through the tee to serve the host structure. Another pipe is connected to the tee and run over to a hot-water tank. From that pipe (the intake), water goes into the hot-water tank, is heated, and then exits the hot-water tank through a different pipe (the discharge).

Water pressure delivered through the main water line goes into the hot water tank to pressurize it. As hot water is drawn from the tank, cold water from the intake line immediately replaces it. This is why cold water comes out of hot-water faucets after your teenagers have taken hour-long showers. The youngsters have used up all of the hot water stored in the hot water tank (which is why the last person in finally got out of the shower).

New hot and cold water service pipes hang just below the ceiling of the garage. They will be placed and secured with pipe holders in the notches cut out of the 2-x-10 floor joists above. To the right is a 1-inch, cold water line teed off the main service that will run over to a hot water tank. It also will be teed at the hot water tank to serve both the tank and the new workshop with cold water.

The ¾-inch hot-water pipe on the left will be teed at the tank. One leg from the tee will carry hot water back toward the house for the home's hot water needs. The other leg of the hot water tee will go to the workshop. Typical freshwater copper pipe sizes are:

1-inch, inside diameter copper pipe	main water supply
¾-inch copper pipe	household distribution lines
½-inch copper pipe	off ¾-inch lines to serve fixtures

Hot & cold freshwater pipes

Fitting pipe through floor joists

Getting long lengths of copper pipe through floor joists is not always easy. Sometimes, you can enlarge an opening on the first joist to allow maneuvering room for pipe to bend and then be pulled through other joists. At other times, it is easier to make access through an exterior wall and route pipes from the outside through holes in successive joists.

The open-ended pipe at the forefront was inserted through the same hole cut in a 2-x-10 block for 2-inch drainpipe. Two 45-degree angle fittings will be used to connect this pipe to the open-ended pipe jutting out from the floor joist ahead of it. This angle in the pipe's routing will keep holes in the floor joists spaced at proper distances. Drainpipe will serve an upstairs vanity and bathtub. Therefore, 3-inch holes were cut in joists for the drainpipe. Holes for copper pipe had to be at least 6 inches away from the drainpipe holes.

Fitting pipe through wall studs

As with floor joists, wall studs can cause problems in routing long pipes. To get pipe from the workshop bathroom to the office area, we drilled holes through all of the bathroom's 2-x-6 wall studs and inserted the pipe from the workshop area. An elbow at this juncture will continue the pipe run.

A felt-tipped pen works great for making cutting marks on pipe. This marked pipe was inserted into a fitting inside the wall to the right. The pipe will not be moved any farther toward the right. The pen mark designates where the pipe should be cut so that it fits snugly inside the elbow and connects to the perpendicular pipe.

After marking the pipe, remove the pipe, cut it, and then attach the elbow by sweating it on. Next, sand the far end of the pipe, flux it, and insert it into its sanded and fluxed fitting inside the wall. The open end of the elbow and the end of the perpendicular pipe also must be sanded, fluxed, and fit together. The elbow must first be sweated onto the perpendicular pipe, then the far end of the pipe must be sweated to its connection inside the 2-x-6 wall.

Soldering

Preparing pipe ends for solder and putting them together before soldering, allows you to make accurate connections before moving on with the project. This ensures that the elbows and tees point in the appropriate, desired direction. If you solder things together without test fitting things first, you'll find that elbows and tees might point down or up inaccurately and will have to be heated up again for removal and repositioning.

Practice with emery cloth, flux, solder, and a propane torch to put together and dismantle copper pipe fittings. While the process is simple, you must use extreme caution when operating a torch. Wood ignites quickly when contacted by a torch flame. Place flame-proof pads behind pipe to protect wood from torch flames. In addition, have a small spray bottle of water on hand to quickly douse wood slivers that ignite. Always have a fire extinguisher handy for any serious fire problems that might develop.

Torch tips

Summary

Although drainpipes will not be subjected to pressure, they must be watertight and airtight to prevent leaks and to prohibit sewer gas from filtering into structural spaces. A local building inspector will inspect your drain system. The main line is plugged and then the system is filled with water through a roof vent. The entire system will be examined for leaks. The system passes inspection when no leaks are detected.

Before hot and cold water distributor lines are connected to actual freshwater supply lines, all half inch outlets and other open lines must be capped. Caps are sweated on and then cut off after drywall operations are completed.

A special connection outfitted to accept an air-pressure gauge and air-filling valve (similar to tire valve stems) must be attached to an open end of your copper pipe system. The entire system is then pressurized to around 80 to 100 psi using an air pump. Air pressure drops signify leaks somewhere in the copper piping.

To detect a leak, fill a small bucket with liquid dishwashing soap and water and use a small paintbrush to dab soap solution onto pipe connections. If the solution bubbles, repair the leak with a torch and solder.

CHAPTER 5

Electricity & lighting

WORKSHOPS NEED to be equipped with plenty of electrical power and lighting. Consult with a representative from your local power company to determine if the main supply to your home will adequately handle the additional needs of your workshop. Plan to have a certified electrician assist you in setting up all of the workshop circuits. Major electrical alterations generally require a building permit. The electrical permit is needed in addition to the permit issued for new construction.

Circuits & circuit breakers

Main electrical service is delivered to households and other structures through a system of high-voltage power lines and substations. Ultimately, electricity arrives at your home or workshop at a meter with a full load of 120 to 200 amperes (amps) or more. Electrical panel boxes are mounted on interior walls (usually right behind meters). Individual circuit breakers or fuses break down the main electrical service into separate circuits with much lower amp ratings. A specific number of outlets, switches, and appliances are served by each circuit.

Attempting to operate too many electrical appliances off one circuit will cause a circuit breaker to trip to the off position and shut down all electricity to that circuit. Circuits are designed to carry a specific ampere load: 15 amps, 20 amps, 30 amps, and up. Normal lighting circuits are set at 15 amps. Regular workshop outlet circuits should be 20 amps. Special 30 amp or larger circuits are dedicated to separate pieces of equipment such as a 220-volt air compressor.

Determining how to set up a workshop with adequate lighting, abundant outlets, and power for special pieces of equipment can be confusing. Decisions are normally based on ampere loads. Circuits are designed to pull no more than 80 percent of a circuit breaker's amp rating. A 20-amp circuit breaker should not have to supply any more than 16 amps (12 amps for a 15-amp breaker, and so on) at one time. Should you consistently tax circuits and circuit breakers with a demand greater than 80 percent of their rating, you risk overheating circuit breakers, wires, and other components.

Ampere load ratings are printed on manufacturer's model number plates on all tools and electric appliances. These plates list how many amps each unit requires for optimum performance. Estimates as to how many 20-amp circuits are needed to power various tools and accessories at the same time is part of overall electrical-circuit equation.

For example, if your table saw requires 12 amps and its dust collector requires 9 amps, you'll need two separate circuits to safely supply both. Consult and work with a certified electrician to ensure that all your workshop's electrical demands are safely and adequately supplied.

Wiring

Electrical wire is available at most home improvement centers, lumberyards, and electrical supply houses. Wire generally is sold in lengths of from 50 feet to 250 feet and is available in different sizes.

The term 14/2 *with ground* refers to a wire size adequate for 15-amp circuits (used mostly for lights). Inside the vinyl covering is a black-coated wire, a white-covered wire, and a bare, ground wire covered with loose paper. Wire labeled 12/2WG (with ground) is suited for 20-amp circuits and also includes a black, white, and ground wire. Wire labeled 14/2 and 12/2 without the "WG" designation signifies no ground wire. Almost all electrical applications call for a ground wire. Use 14/2WG for lights and 12/2WG for receptacles.

Inexpensive plastic switch and receptacle boxes must be secured in position before wire is strung. Most boxes are equipped with nails snugly inserted into holders. Hold them against a stud and drive in the nails. Workshops are generally served best with receptacles mounted at about 4 feet from the floor, plainly in view and accessible. Receptacles mounted low to the floor, like in other areas of the house, would make the receptacles tough to reach behind workbenches, power equipment, and other obstacles.

Receptacles

Workshops can almost never have too many receptacles. Plan to install at least one receptacle every 4 feet or so. While installing boxes, use a piece of ½-inch drywall as a guide. Boxes should stick out past studs flush to the drywall.

Circuit wires must run from a circuit breaker at the electrical panel through walls, perhaps to a second story, through floor joists areas or attics, to workshop areas, and then to light switches, lights, or receptacles. A series of 1-inch holes must be drilled in studs, wall plates, or joists in order to provide routes for the wire.

The electrical code limits the number of wires that can be routed through any hole made through studs, wall plates, or joists to three. Code also mandates a maximum of two wires secured by any one staple.

All together, four wires run to a two-gang box below. This electrical receptacle box holds two receptacles for a total of four plugs. Because two holes had to be drilled in the wall's top plate and only two wires could be secured by one staple, it was easiest to route each two-wire line through separate holes. Notice that these wires are centered in the middle of the 2-x-6 wall stud. This was done to keep them at least 1½ inches away from the nailing face of the stud so that they would not be damaged by drywall nails or screws that veer off the side of the stud.

Wires have been routed low to the wall's bottom plate to make it easier to install insulation. Had the wiring been located in the middle of the wall, maneuvering insulation around the wires would have been cumbersome. Note that brown- and ivory-colored receptacles are installed in the box on the right. This box has been wired and is in use even though insulation and drywall operations are not completed. This was done to provide interim workshop power.

To clearly identify the four separate electrical circuits that will serve this workshop, Steve Brown, our son-in-law electrician, suggested we outfit circuit A with ivory-colored receptacles, circuit B with brown, circuit C with white, and circuit D with gray. The receptacle sequence around the shop would follow an A, B, C, D circuit pattern. This way, if more than one person works in the shop, everyone will have their own circuit, avoiding overloading any one circuit.

Extra studs placed at the corner of workshops frequently pose wire-routing problems. Sometimes, it is easier to go up through a wall and ceiling. Note that a maximum of two wires are secured with single staples and wires neatly placed in the center of studs, plates, and joists.

Nailing plates are crucially important for all wires that rest closer than 1½ inches to the nailing faces of studs, plates, joists,

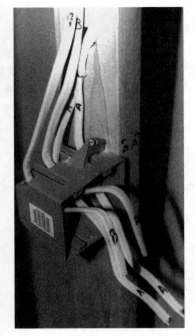

and so on. Should you neglect to install nailing plates over wires resting closer to stud nailing faces, you risk a very real chance of driving drywall nails or screws into wires.

With wiring yet to be connected to a circuit breaker and power waiting to be supplied to wiring until after drywall work has been completed, you might not discover that drywall nails or screws driven into wiring until power is turned on and circuits suffer direct shorts or a fire starts. Nailing plates are very inexpensive and there is no excuse for not using plenty of them throughout your workshop.

Wiring route

Typically, wire starts out at the circuit breaker and is routed to the first receptacle on a circuit. A length of wire about 6 to 8 inches long is allowed to stick out of the box. That length will be used later to make up the connection to a receptacle. Wire is also left at the box and run to the next box served on the circuit. The series continues until all circuit boxes are supplied with wire.

In essence, a single wire stretches from a circuit breaker to all boxes on the circuit terminating at the last box on the line. For ease of maneuvering, wire is cut at each box and then routed to the next. At each point where wire is cut, it must be connected to a receptacle. Power will come in on one line and go into the receptacle. The next wire connects to the receptacle and then carries electricity to the next box, and so on. The last box on the circuit will have only one wire coming into it with nothing going out.

On the right is a *ground fault circuit interrupter* (GFCI). On the left is a standard receptacle. In bathrooms and kitchens, GFCIs are excellent safety devices required for all receptacles located near any water source. The GFCI immediately will react to shut off power any time an abnormal change in electrical current is sensed. Their reaction time is much faster than circuit breakers or fuses. In addition to reacting faster, GFCIs are also capable of reacting to more electrical irregularities than circuit breakers or fuses.

We decided to wire in GFCI units as the very first receptacles in line for all of our workshop circuits. A GFCI unit correctly wired

Ground fault circuit interrupters

in as the first receptacle on a circuit will also protect all of the other receptacles on that circuit.

The Power Tool Institute recommends that all power tools be protected by GFCIs. Along with GFCI receptacles, GFCI extension cords and other devices are available through many home-improvement centers and electrical-supply houses. For information about power-tool safety and workshop safety, write to the Power Tool Institute at the address listed in the Sources.

Making wire connections

Electrical wiring labeled 12/2WG includes black, white, and bare ground wires. All three wires play important roles in overall electric service. CAUTION: Never attempt to adjust, tighten, or fool around with any electrical wire until all power has been shut off to it. It only takes a very small amount of electricity conducted under just the right circumstances to kill. Normal workshop electrical current is enough to prove fatal.

As is illustrated by this Leviton receptacle, almost all electrical receptacles designate to which terminal you should connect the white wires. Regular receptacles have two screws on one side, two screws on the other, and a single green screw at the bottom. Only the very last receptacle on a circuit has just one black, white, and ground wire to attach. Others in the circuit will have two of each; one brings in the electricity and one takes it to the next receptacle.

Hook up the white wires to the side designated with the word "White" next to it. The black wires go on the other side. Ground (green) screws typically are designed to accept one wire. Therefore, you have to twist ground wires together, crimp them together with a special little ground wire clip, and then attach one of the two ground wires to the receptacle's ground screw.

Wires are connected to light switches differently than receptacles. Their function is to cut power to lights when switched off. Wiring runs from the power supply (circuit breaker) to the switch and from the switch to lights. Except for those applications where more than one switch controls lights (called two-way, three-way, and four-way switches), black wires coming from the breaker and going to the light(s) are the only ones connected to the switch. The white wires are connected directly together and secured with a wire nut; the same is true with the ground wires.

Lights

Home workshops demand plenty of illumination. Working in dimly lit conditions is simply an accident waiting to happen. Without sufficient light, you will have a difficult time putting

small project parts together, seeing cut lines on boards, noticing tripping hazards before you trip, and so on.

Recessed lighting

Recessed (can) lights work fine for small workshops requiring direct light for specific needs. An example would be a small workbench area for electronics repair or hobbyist activities. Recessed lights are equipped with arms that attach with nails or screws, to ceiling joists. Once arms are secure, light fixtures can be adjusted back and forth to desired positions.

Fluorescent lighting

Workshops are well served with fluorescent light. Fluorescent bulbs put out a different type of light than incandescent bulbs. Incandescent light concentrates light on a particular area and tends to cast shadows. Fluorescent light spreads out and greatly reduces images.

SIMKAR and Power Products Company offer numerous types and styles of fluorescent lighting. In order for our workshop to maintain an 8-foot, 2-inch-plus ceiling level, we needed fixtures that would fit flush to the ceiling and between floor joists set at 16 inches on center. The adjustable support arms for our lights featured an angled end section designed to rest on top of ceiling drywall.

Because the workshop's ceiling joists were wood I-beam trusses that sported small lips at their bases, I decided to alter the lights' supports so that they could be screwed directly into the wood I-beams. First, I cut off about a half inch (the angled portion) from each light fixture support. Next, I drilled holes in the ends for mounting screws.

Support brackets were assembled onto light fixtures and adjusted to their lowest hanging point to accommodate ceiling drywall installation. Note the electrical wire mount located on the middle section of the fixture's near end. Romex 14/2WG wire will be inserted into this connection and secured with screws and a crossbar mechanism, which will run to the light fixture positioned in line with this one.

In order to hang lights in a straight line, a string was positioned and secured with nails along the bottom edge of the ceiling/floor joists. String serves as a guide to designate where the ends of each light should rest.

A cordless drill was used to cinch down screws that support light-fixture brackets. Without that tool, we would have had to use a small screwdriver, and it would have taken us a great deal longer to install the lights.

Lips on both sides of the light fixture will eventually meet with ceiling drywall. Long screws to which mounting brackets are attached are accessed from the face of the fixture and adjusted until the fixture makes contact with the drywall surface. Additional trim pieces included with the fixture will be assembled onto the narrow sides to complete the installation.

These fluorescent light units feature a black wire, a white wire, and a ground wire screw. For this workshop's application, I ran power to the lights on one side and then connected the other lights end to end.

As you can see, Romex wire was used to power these lights. The first unit in line handles two 14/2WG wires; one comes from the switch and the other powers the rest of the lights. A short piece of wire was used to connect the first light to the one next to it. All wiring inside lights will be covered with a metal shield before bulbs are put in.

To ensure adequate illumination, we installed eight 4-foot, 2-bulb fluorescent light fixtures per 300 square feet of floor area. It was a wise decision. It's a real pleasure working in there.

Summary

Outfitting workshops with electricity and lights must not be taken lightly. Other than a roof over your head and a place where you can work out of the weather, workshops must provide users with enough power to effectively operate different tools and equipment. If you began your do-it-yourself endeavors on the back porch of an old house with just one two-prong electrical receptacle and a single bulb light fixture, you'll know what I mean.

It is a pleasure working in a shop that is brightly illuminated and has enough electrical power so that two or three tools can be operated simultaneously. Unless you've had extensive experience working with electricity to know the best way to put an entire workshop's electrical system together safely and efficiently, I recommend you consult with a professional.

We are lucky. Steve, our son-in-law electrician, was delighted to help out. He is looking forward to using our family workshop, too. Do you have any friends or family members who are electricians? If you're a handy do-it-yourselfer, maybe you can swap labor. That's what Mike Holiman did. Because he is an ace auto mechanic, Mike did a lot of automotive work for friends in trade for their expertise and help building his home workshop.

Interior finishings

JOHN GITTINGS has completed hundreds of projects in his giant workshop that is unfinished and still features a dirt floor. Many do-it-yourselfers successfully complete projects in drafty outbuildings that have bare stud walls and uneven floors. Although simple workshops might suffice by keeping users out of the weather, you will have to admit that finished walls, ceilings, and floors go a long way toward making all workshops more comfortable and inviting. Be patient. Hold off moving your tools and other treasures into your workshop until interior finish work is completed.

Floors

Small workshops built in vacant bedrooms or other household areas might be well served with carpet. Work undertaken in carpeted areas must be confined to clean operations such as electronics repair and small-appliance repair. Woodworking projects result in sawdust debris that is difficult to remove from carpeting. If your plans include woodworking and other debris-producing endeavors, consider hardwood or vinyl flooring.

Concrete floors

Concrete floors are virtually maintenance free, hold up well under most workshop conditions, and offer solid surfaces on which to work. For cabinet building and other projects, spend extra time ensuring that your concrete floors are flat, smooth, and even.

Rough spots on concrete surfaces are signs of an uneven finish. Light colored and rough looking spots on our workshop floor are located on both sides of a metal-expansion joint. The expansion joint rests directly beneath a hairline crack, which is typical for expansion joints. Some DAP latex-fortified cement patching compound can be used to fill in and even out low spots. Afterward, the entire floor will be sealed with a concrete sealer and might even get a paint job with an epoxy, concrete floor paint.

Wood floors

Wood floors in older homes sometimes suffer squeaks, buckles, weak spots, and other problems. Should you decide to completely remodel an old bedroom, den, or rumpus room into a first-class workshop, plan to rebuild the old, rickety floor.

Wood floors generally consist of two parts: a basic subfloor of 1x boards or ¾-inch plywood and a second layer of ½-inch particleboard or ¾-inch hardwood. The ½-inch particleboard must be covered with floor vinyl or carpet. Hardwood flooring is applied, then sanded, and sealed.

Subflooring

If you plan to install new underlayment, first remove the old and damaged subflooring so you can repair the basic subfloor. The subfloor must be clean before installing building paper and particleboard.

After all damaged sections of the first subfloor have been replaced with new wood and all boards are securely anchored to floor joists with deck screws, a layer of 15-pound building paper is stapled in place. Particleboard rated as "floor underlayment" is then anchored through the subfloor and into floor joists with deck screws. Straight chalk lines indicate floor joist positions as a guide for floor screws. The entire surface must be smooth and even before floor vinyl can be glued into position. If any seams or gaps appear, the floor underlayment must be filled with patching material.

Building departments typically require wall and ceiling insulation for all heated structures. Owens-Corning offers fiberglass insulation in sizes to fit all walls and ceiling spaces. The R values, which rate its insulation properties, vary according to material thickness and style. In general, thicker materials offer higher R-values. However, don't try to stuff R-21, 5½ inch insulation into 2-x-4 wall spaces in hopes of increasing the insulating value. Compacting insulation reduces its efficiency.

Plan to wear long sleeves, gloves, and safety goggles whenever you are working with insulation. Although fiberglass insulation is available in various batt lengths, there are times you must cut it to fit certain wall cavities, such as under windows, or separate them to fit around obstructions such as electrical wiring.

Use a sharp utility knife to score the paper moisture barrier, then use a straight piece of wood or a steel square as a guide to cut the remaining material. Lay a piece of plywood down on the floor to serve as a base so that the blade doesn't scar the floor surface. This helps to keep your knife sharp, too.

Insulation

Had these wires been positioned in the middle of the wall, installing insulation would have been difficult. Wires at this level make it easy to separate insulation layers and fit half behind wires and half in front. Flaps on each side of insulation batts fold out and are stapled to wall studs as a means to hold insulation in place. A utility knife is also used to cut away sections of insulation so that batts will fit around electrical boxes.

Insulation for ceilings is thicker than that for walls. To make it easier to install, ceiling insulation batts are available in 4-foot lengths. The ceiling insulation is also secured to joists by stapling paper flaps to them.

Wall coverings

After insulation is installed, walls can be covered with drywall, T1-11 plywood, sheets of 4-x-8-foot wood paneling, pegboard, 1x boards, or a combination of materials.

Wood wall coverings

The Western Wood Products Association and the American Plywood Association offer numerous guidelines regarding the installation, sealing, and staining or painting of various wood wall coverings.

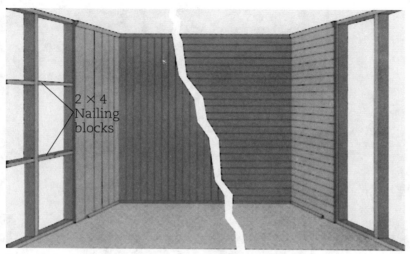

For vertical paneling, use nailing blocks between studs (illustrated) or furring strips applied to face of studs. For horizontal paneling, position joints over studs to provide nailing base. Use random length boards so joints are staggered.

Wood-covered walls provide an aesthetically pleasing and warm environment. Should you decide to install wood, stain it a light color to enhance overall illumination. Dark walls absorb a great deal of light and can reduce the effectiveness of general lighting.

Drywall

Drywall is inexpensive and available in 4-foot widths and 8-to-12-foot lengths. All ceilings and walls that separate workshops and garages from living spaces must be covered with ⅝-inch drywall. Other walls are covered with ½-inch drywall.

The easiest way to install drywall on ceilings and upper walls is with a PanelLift Telpro drywall lift. If you have ever had to hold up and secure sheets of ⅝-inch ceiling drywall, you can truly appreciate this piece of equipment. The PanelLift is fully adjustable to accommodate all drywall lengths. Wide-spanning legs offer plenty of support and large wheels at their ends make the unit easy to maneuver.

Seldom will you be able to install full sheets of drywall. Pieces must be cut to fit around electrical boxes, windows, door

openings, and so on. You will need a tape measure, a pencil, a cutting guide, and a sharp, straightedge utility knife for drywall cutting and fitting tasks.

Measuring & cutting drywall

Take your time accurately measuring and transferring marks onto drywall sheets. Careful attention to detail during this process saves work later when it comes time to mud and tape seams, and when you install window and door trim.

Drywall is designed with front and back faces. Back faces are designed to be placed against studs and generally feature a darker paper surface. Front faces are lighter in color and feature a definitive taper along edges. Edges are actually thinner than the rest of the sheet. Tapers allow extra room for the addition of drywall tape and mud.

Make all your pencil marks on front drywall faces. Score lines with three or four passes of a sharp utility knife. Then, turn sheets on their edge and snap them at the scoring mark.

Drywall will bend at that point and all you will have to do is cut the back face paper to completely separate pieces.

Drywall cutting bits are available for use with Makita trimmer tools. Many professionals use trimmers to cut out drywall pieces. You must practice with these tools first before using them for actual drywall projects.

Before installing drywall over concrete foundations, concrete must be smoothed with all protruding imperfections removed. Makita's Concrete Planer makes quick work of these chores. Because drywall nails or screws cannot secure drywall to concrete, use DAP drywall adhesive.

Installing drywall

Many installers prefer to keep drywall off actual floor surfaces. You can accomplish this by simply placing drywall on top of a thin piece of wood or lath. Rest drywall on top of the spacer while driving nails or drywall screws. Pull out the spacer once the drywall is secured.

Drywall is attached to wall and ceiling studs with drywall screws or special drywall nails. Both types of fasteners must be driven into the drywall so that their heads actually rest under the drywall surface. Drywall mud is used to cover up the nail and screw heads.

Makita's drywall screwdriver is fully adjustable to accurately set drywall screws uniformly. A magnetic bit holds screws in place while you are positioning the tool. It drives screws quickly and helps users to finish drywall installations in a fraction of the time it takes to pound drywall nails with a hammer.

Drywall nails feature cupped heads designed to allow room for drywall mud. Like drywall screws, nails must be set below drywall surfaces to make room for mud.

The Stanley Goldblatt Drywall Hammer is specially designed with a rounded hammer head to drive nails below drywall surfaces and dimple drywall surfaces so mud can be applied. NOTE: If a nail misses a stud, pull it out and install another nail. Otherwise, it will eventually pop out of the wall and mar the overall finish. In lieu of extracting loose nails, drive a second one into the stud with its head positioned over part of the other.

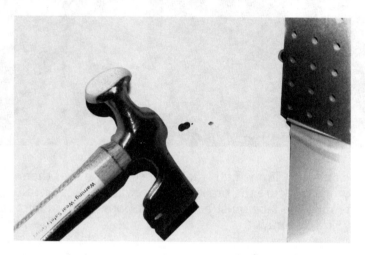

Drywall nails, screws, seams, and joints must be covered with drywall mud and tape for smooth finishes. Expect to apply three coats of mud over the course of at least three days. Each coat must cure before another is added.

Finishing drywall

Drywall mud is applied with a tool that looks a lot like an extra-wide putty knife. Mud alone is applied over all screws or nails. Apply a combination of mud and tape for seams, gaps, and joints. Be certain all nails or screws have been driven below drywall surfaces or mud will not adequately cover them.

A first coat of mud is applied with a 6-inch-wide blade to initially fill all depressed areas. Apply mud to seams, gaps, and

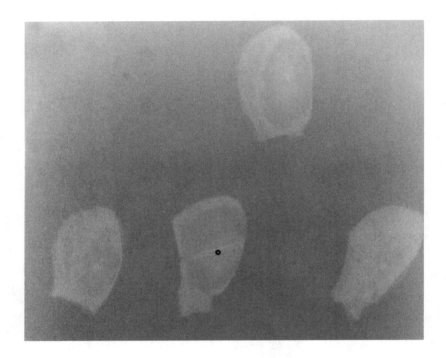

joints and then immediately lay a piece of tape over them. Smooth and secure the tape with a drywall applicator full of fresh mud. The tape must become wet from the mud in order to lay down evenly.

Notice the tapered edge on the top drywall section. Fresh mud will be covered with tape as soon as the entire length is filled. Two sections of tape are needed—one for each seam.

Inside & outside corners

Inside corners are easiest to apply mud to and tape with this type of drywall corner tool. Notice that tape has been secured at the top and hangs loose at the bottom. Excess mud from outer edges is removed after the tape is affixed.

Outside drywall corners are covered with a metal strip designed for that application. Strips are shaped at right angles and simply nailed into position. They are then covered with mud just like all other joints.

After the first coat of drywall mud has dried, use a drywall knife to scrape away globs of excess mud. Then apply a thin, second coat using a wider (8 to 10 inches) applicator. Once it dries, scrape off excess mud as you did before and then apply a third coat using *drywall finish mud* and an even bigger (about 12 inches wide) applicator. Once that final coat has dried, sand all surfaces to a smooth finish.

Pegboard

Pegboard is available in sheets measuring 4 × 8 feet. For workshops, plan to use ¼-inch-thick material. Pegboard must have an open space behind it about ⅛ to ¼ inch deep in order to allow room for hooks.

Strips of wood called *furring* are nailed or screwed over flat walls and into studs to serve as backing for pegboard. At the same time, the furring strips allow for open spaces for pegboard hooks.

Some do-it-yourselfers find that covering entire workshop walls with ¼-inch pegboard offers them a multitude of choices for openly storing tools and other items. Others prefer just a few pegboard sites typically located near workbenches and power equipment such as lathes, shapers, and drill presses. Pegboard panels on cabinet doors make fine places for storing saw blades and other small accessories.

Paint and stain

Vic Lopez from the Behr Process Corporation contends that about 95 percent of the problems associated with paint and stain applications are generally a direct result of users not following the directions featured on product labels. A great amount of research goes into the development of all paint and stain products. Explicit directions on cans of paint and stain fully explain how surfaces are supposed to be prepared before the actual application of any paint or stain material.

In almost every case, bare surfaces—such as wood, drywall, plaster, and the like—must be sealed before being painted or stained. If you expect the paint or stain finish in your workshop to look great and stay that way for a long time, pay attention to and follow manufacturer's preparation and application directions.

All finishing nails used to secure wood trim around windows and doors should be driven below wood surfaces with a nail set and holes filled with wood putty. The idea is to make the wood appear to have no nails in them at all. Wood putty is also used to fill gaps typically located at mitered corners.

CHAPTER 7

Workbenches & storage

HOME WORKSHOPS offer ideal spaces for the storage of tools, equipment, materials, and supplies. Building workbenches and storage units gives you opportunities to actually work in your workshop. This activity should help you plan and decide how you eventually want to set up the workshop's tool, equipment, and general floor plan.

Workbenches

Even the fanciest and most fully stocked workbench will not comfortably serve you if it sets too high or too low, and is too wide or too narrow. Design workbenches with dimensions that fit your personal height and arm reach.

Workbench heights of 36 to 38 inches are ideal for persons who stand about 6 feet tall. Do-it-yourselfers who don't quite reach 6 feet are best served with workbenches set just below belt level. Home workshops should be set up with separate-workbench areas designed for children and built to their size requirements. Working at heights commensurate with their size, children are able to work more safely. Generally consider the following height guidelines:

Workbench	3 to 4 inches below belt line
Sawhorse	around knee-high
Radial arm saw unit	waist-high
Table saw	3 to 4 inches below belt line
Top shelves	1 foot below extended arm reach

Workbenches do not have to conform to any specific style or design. Although some basic factors must be taken into account—like strength, convenience, and accessory features—build anything you want, as long as it satisfies your needs.

74   *The Complete Home Workshop*

Workbenches & storage   75

To make a handy chop-saw workbench, you can nail 2 × 4s to open wall studs to support 2-×-6 boards. I built a temporary unit to accommodate work involved with a new door installation and other remodeling. If your garage or workshop features bare-studded walls, this type of workbench might be fine. Nail 2 × 4s of a desired length to every stud along the length of your proposed workbench.

Determine an appropriate brace length and cut both ends of each board at a 45-degree angle. Nail one end of each brace to studs and then toenail the other end to the bottom of horizontal 2 × 4s. Cover the top with 2× material.

Lots of various workbench styles are available for purchase through home-improvement centers, lumberyards, and woodworking-supply stores. This unit from Harbor Freight Tools is especially designed for woodworking. Matt, Nick, and Adam took just a few minutes to assemble the workbench using its packaged nuts and bolts. Two woodworking vises are also provided with this model. They attach at each end of the unit.

In addition to finding ready-made workbenches through retail outlets, consider building your own workbench from plans made available through the Western Wood Products Association and the American Plywood Association.

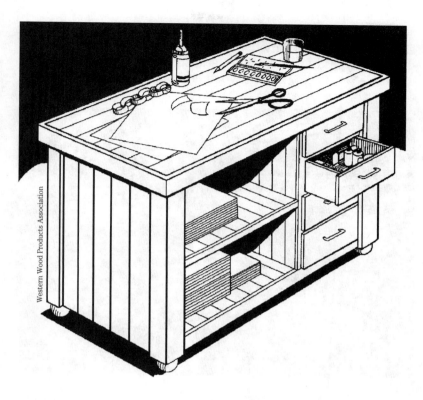

Western Wood Products Association

Materials list

(lumber shown in linear feet)
1 × 1, 22'
1 × 2, 40'
1 × 4, 195'
1 × 6, 15'
1 × 8, 30'
2 × 2, 30'
2 × 4, 10'
4 × 4, 11'
Nails: 3d (11/4"); 4d (11/2");
6d (2"); 10d (3')
(4) drawer pulls
1 3/4" or longer machine
screws (for drawer pulls)
See note. step 27.
(4) locking swivel casters
Carpenter's glue

CAUTION: Be certain that you review and understand all steps of construction and verify all dimensions before cutting your material. While every effort has been made to ensure accuracy in the design and drawing of all WWPA plans, the possibilty of error always exists and WWPA cannot accept responsibility for lumber improperly used or designs not first verified.

The illustration and materials list from WWPA Plan Sheet 61 shows how to build a mobile workbench. Other plans for different types of workbenches and storage units are also available from the Western Wood Productions Association.

Workbenches designed for specific uses are commonly custom made for individual tools or pieces of equipment. A table was constructed out of 2 × 4s and plywood to support our compound saw that is bolted to the table. A 2-×-4 extension table is outfitted with a 2 × 6 nailed to the top to serve as a guide. Consider a workbench with a dropped section in it as a permanent option for a chop-saw workbench.

The workbench pictured on the top of the page is a permanent workbench set up for the Makita Slide Compound Saw at Logan Lumber Company's cabinet shop in Seattle. A Vise-Grip tool to the right holds a wood block securely in position. This block is used as a stop for operations that call for many pieces of wood to be cut at exactly the same length. Note how the saw's support is located below workbench level so that wood can slide from one workbench to the other along the saw's base.

This handy wood-scrap-and-sawdust collection box was built on casters and placed under the chop saw. Notice that both workbenches have notches cut into them to accommodate the saw's rotating base plate.

Solid, 36-inch upright 2 × 4s support other 2 × 4s to make up a workbench frame. Quick-Grip bar clamps are holding the unit together while a cross brace is nailed to the front and rear 2-x-4 uprights. Later, ¾-inch plywood will be notched to fit on top of these lower 2-x-4 supports for a bottom shelf. Horizontal 2 × 4s across the top will support another piece of ¾-inch plywood for a workbench top. A workbench like this can be made, at any length, with legs spaced no more than 4 feet apart.

Workbench legs can be made from 2 × 4s, 4 × 4s, plywood, angle iron, or anything you want that is strong enough to support the weight placed on it.

No workshop is complete without a pair of sawhorses. Dennis Fortier from Logan Lumber Company's cabinet shop was taught this design by his high school shop teacher. The sawhorses were made with a 2-x-6 top piece and ¾-inch plywood legs and gussets.

Plywood is cut in strips about 8 inches wide for the legs. Note that the table saw is plugged into an ivory-colored receptacle and the dust collector is connected to a brown receptacle. Both units are powered by separate circuits. Therefore, I have no worries about electrical overloading or tripping circuit breakers.

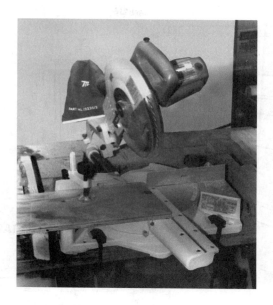

Also, note the handy roller stand located behind the saw. The stand supports the plywood as it goes past the end of the table saw.

All angles for this sawhorse design are set at 12 degrees. Our slide compound saw was set to cut both vertically and horizontally at 12 degrees. The first item to cut was a plywood leg top. After that cut, the next step was to slide the board across the saw table until reaching the 30-inch mark. At that point, an identical cut was made. This resulted in two 12-degree cuts at both ends that will be just the opposite of each other once the board is nailed to the 2-x-6 top piece.

Both sides of the 2 × 6 were cut at 12 degrees on the table saw. As you can see, having cut the sawhorse legs in the manner just described, the top sections rest flush at 12 degree angles pointing one way while the bottoms rest flush at 12 degrees pointing the other.

After the sawhorse legs are attached to 2 × 6s, plywood gussets were stapled to both their inside and outside faces. Gussets add a great deal of strength to these sawhorses. Without them, they would not be able to support anything.

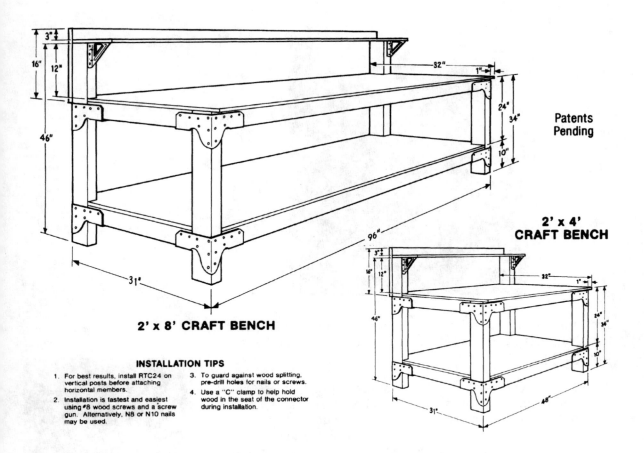

2' x 8' CRAFT BENCH

2' x 4' CRAFT BENCH

Patents Pending

INSTALLATION TIPS

1. For best results, install RTC24 on vertical posts before attaching horizontal members.

2. Installation is fastest and easiest using #8 wood screws and a screw gun. Alternatively, N8 or N10 nails may be used.

3. To guard against wood splitting, pre-drill holes for nails or screws.

4. Use a "C" clamp to help hold wood in the seat of the connector during installation.

CRAFT BENCH, MATERIALS LIST

SIZE	MATERIAL	LENGTH	4' BENCH QUANTITY	8' BENCH QUANTITY
2"x 4"	Douglas Fir	8'	5 ea.	9 ea.
3/4"	Plywood, 4'x 8'	—	1 Sheet	2 Sheets
	Simpson RTC24		8	8
	Simpson CF		2	2
	Simpson SD8x1.25		200	200

CRAFT BENCH, CUT LIST (Maximizes material use)

DESCRIPTION	QUANTITY	SIZE	CUT LENGTH 4' BENCH	CUT LENGTH 8' BENCH
Back Legs	2	2"x 4"	46"	46"
Front Legs	2	2"x 4"	33-1/2"	33-1/2"
Rails	4	2"x 4"	45"	93"
Side Rails	4	2"x 4"	24"	24"
Plywood Top	2	3/4" Plywood	32"x 48"	32"x 96"
Plywood Shelf	1	3/4" Plywood	10"x 48"	10"x 96"
Back Stop	1	3/4" Plywood	16"x 48"	16"x 96"
Simpson RTC24	8	N.A.		
Simpson CF	2	N.A.		
Simpson SD8x1.25	160	#8 x 1-1/4" Screw		

Note: Dimensions and cut list are suggested only; plans may be modified to suit your requirements.

The Simpson Strong-Tie Company has developed a workbench design that makes use of their Rigid-Tie corner connectors. Bar clamps and a cordless drill made easy work of attaching the corner connectors to the 2 × 4s.

The rear upright 2 × 4s were allowed to extend past the workbench top to serve as a shelf support. Cordless saws were used to notch the plywood so the plywood would fit around the 2 × 4. The workbench's lower ¾-inch plywood shelf was notched at all four corners so it could fit around the upright supports.

The square front corners of the workbench were rounded off with a cordless jigsaw to keep sharp corners from being a hazard. A quart can was used as a guide to make a pencil mark around the corner of the workbench top. The jigsaw was maneuvered along that line to produce the rounded corner.

Simpson shelf brackets attached to the upper portion of the rear 2-x-4 uprights make for a handy shelf support. A small back support for the top shelf was made with ¾-inch plywood to keep objects from being knocked off the back of the shelf.

While the tops of shelf ends make perfect storage spots for an assortment of bar clamps, ¼-inch pegboard is ideal for holding tools. In addition, a strong lower shelf is the best area for heavy storage.

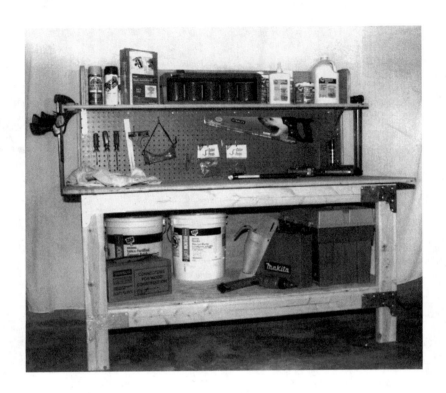

In short time, home workshops are frequently dubbed family warehouses. It seems like everything under the sun eventually gets tossed into whatever space is available. If your detached workshop has attic space, invest in an Attic Stairway from Keller. The unit simply pulls down and unfolds from the ceiling to offer a sturdy stairway to attic spaces.

Utility shelfs

In addition to attic storage, consider every available open workshop area for possible storage. An easy-to-build utility shelf can be made from 2 × 4s, 1 × 4s, and 1 × 10s or 1 × 12s. The Western Wood Products Association has a variety of storage-unit plans available.

If the ceiling in your workshop has been covered with drywall, use lag bolts to secure 2 × 2s to ceiling joists. The 2 × 2s will rest flush against the drywall while lag bolts go through the 2 × 2s, the drywall, and into the joists.

UTILITY SHELVES

(Plans courtesy Georgia-Pacific)

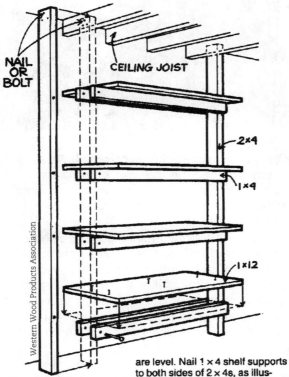

NAIL OR BOLT

CEILING JOIST

2×4

1×4

1×12

Western Wood Products Association

Here's a handy shelf unit that's exceptionally easy to build. Because of the sturdy T-style design of the shelf support, shelves may be up to 8' long.

1—To determine length of 2 × 4s, measure distance between floor and ceiling joist and add at least 3" for overlap.

2—Temporarily nail 2 × 4s in place and check with a level to make sure they are vertical. Finish nailing 2 × 4s to joists, using (3) nails per 2 × 4.

3—Mark location of shelves on vertical 2 × 4s, making sure shelves are level. Nail 1 × 4 shelf supports to both sides of 2 × 4s, as illustrated. (If unit is too close to wall to nail shelf supports, drill ¼" holes through all thicknesses and secure with 5½" carriage bolts.) Nail shelves to 1 × 4 supports with 8d nails.

Materials List for Utility Shelves

Uprights: (2) 2 × 4s
Shelf supports: (2) 1 × 4s per shelf
Shelves: 1 × 10 or 1 × 12, up to 8' long
Nails: 6d, 8d
Bolts: (optional) 5½" carriage bolts

These brackets were mounted high on a wall. They extend over a doorway to the right. Out of the way up on a wall, wood molding and trim pieces are protected against accidental damage and won't interfere with other workshop activities.

Wood storage

Wood storage is a common workshop storage dilemma. Most do-it-yourselfers are classic pack rats who have trouble tossing anything—especially pieces of expensive hardwood—into the trash. An under-the-workbench, wood-storage system could hold lots of wood lengthwise and in bundles according to wood species. Plywood storage is another problem frequently faced by do-it-yourselfers. Ideally, plywood should be stored flat. Unfortunately, that takes up a lot of room.

Bins like the one shown on the bottom of the opposite page can work well for large workshops with plenty of room. For smaller workshops, you will just have to limit the amount of plywood you keep on hand. Another way to accommodate plywood storage is to leave a void between walls and the back sides of workbenches where plywood can be slipped into and stood upright on either a 4-foot or 8-foot side, depending upon your workshop's ceiling height.

Lots of ideas and plans are available for the constructing of wood shelves, bins, and storage units. Along with the sources listed at the back of this book, look through home improvement and woodworking magazines for ideas.

Summary

Matt, Nick, Adam, and Luke, are just about finished putting together a 6-foot-tall shelf unit from Plano. This model simply snaps together in a matter of minutes. Cylindrical tube supports can be cut to any height and lips at the rear of each shelf feature holes through which screws are driven into studs to keep units from being accidentally knocked over.

Workshop storage is all encompassing. You'll need storage bins, units, and containers of all kinds. As you go about outfitting your workshop, force yourself to separate the contents of generic containers and put them into compartmentalized units. You will thank yourself later when it doesn't take you a half an hour to find those wood screws you know are tucked away somewhere.

CHAPTER 8

Cabinets, cupboards, & drawers

ALONG WITH or instead of open shelves and racks, you might want to outfit your workshop with a series of cabinets, cupboards, and drawers. In this chapter, consider cabinets deep, from floor level up to waist-high with hinged doors. Cupboards are upper storage compartments located above work counters, about a foot deep, with hinged doors. Drawers serve the cabinets; otherwise, there would be no way to see inside them if they were mounted in cupboards.

Cabinets and cupboards can be constructed out of any wood material. ACX plywood makes excellent shelves and side panels, while birch, oak, or other hardwood plywood works best for doors and panels that will be visible. Hardwood plywood accepts stain and paint much better than standard plywood, and it doesn't have as many problems related to buckling and warping.

The set of cabinets pictured on the opposite page is just a part of Jim Yocum's overall garage/workshop plan. The unit on the right is designed for garden tool storage and will receive two full-length doors. Together, there are three separate units connected to the garage wall. In the back, they are connected to the wall with long screws; to each other, they are connected with screws through the front trim pieces.

The upper cupboards in Jim's garage are built and assembled with ACX plywood for sides and shelves, a hardboard backing, clear fir trim (rails and stiles), and birch plywood doors. Notice the rabbet edge around door edges. This indentation allows a portion of each door to actually fit inside an opening and help seal off interiors from sawdust and other airborne debris.

To take full advantage of plywood sheets, cabinets were designed to be 2 feet wide and cupboards are 1 foot wide. Cabinet countertops are cut a bit wider to offer a front lip for clamps.

Dimensions

For your own units, spend plenty of time figuring out the dimensions for cabinets and cupboards. You must account for the depth of dado cuts or router grooves. Generally, the depth will be about ⅜ inch deep (half the width of ¾-inch plywood). For example, if you want to build 4-foot-wide units, interior shelves must not measure any longer than 3 feet ¼ inch. If the shelves are not the correct length, a section of 4-foot-wide hardboard cannot span the full distance across the back of the units, and you would have 4-foot shelves mounted inside dado cuts or router grooves that are only ⅜ of an inch deep into the ¾-inch side members. The remaining ⅜ inch on each side panel will bring the entire unit width to 4 feet ¾ inches.

Constructing panels

Cabinet side panels should have dado cuts or router grooves installed 4 inches from the floor, in the center, and along the top edge. Horizontal shelves are glued and screwed into these grooves.

A vertical pencil line on this ¾-inch side panel (the unit is on its back on the floor) shows where a ¾-inch shelf has been inserted into a ¾-inch groove on the panel's inside face. Screws hold the shelf in place. On the plywood edge, clear Douglas fir trim has been glued and secured with finish nails.

Notice that a 3½-x-3½-inch notch has been cut out of each lower corner and that the bottom face of the lowest shelf sits at the 3½-inch mark. The notch and accompanying open space at the front base of the unit is standard. The notch makes room for a person to stand and work as well as room to reach for objects inside the cabinets. Two 2 × 4s have been nailed to the lower sections of the side panels to serve as unit supports. A full sheet of hardboard has been nailed using finishing nails to the back of the unit.

Jim uses a Stanley hand drill to make pilot holes in trim wood before securing the trim with finishing nails. Pilot holes help prevent wood from splitting. A ¾-inch-thick trim—about 1½ to 2 inches wide—is placed flush with the top of the lid and flush with the bottom shelf's top surface; trim overlaps downward.

Installing trim

On the sides, trim is allowed to hang over the outside edge about ¾ of an inch. When separate modules are positioned together side by side, only those side trim pieces will actually touch. An air space will exist between the plywood sides.

Cabinets are built this way so they can be positioned flush to each other, side by side, as viewed from the front. The space

between plywood side panels allows some room for adjustment. Floors are not always flat and units will not always fit together flush as expected.

Jim has trimmed out the top, bottom, and sides of this cabinet module and is now installing a trim piece in the center of the unit. Another will be positioned above this one. Note the block of wood support at the base and the bar clamp employed to keep the trim piece flush against the piece to which it is being attached.

On its back with Jim standing inside the upper portion of the cabinet, finish nails are toenailed into the bottom of an upper middle trim piece. These upright trim pieces located in the center of this 4-foot-wide unit help support shelves and also serve as stops for hinged cabinet doors.

This module measures exactly 4 feet wide from outside plywood panel to outside plywood panel. From the outside of

each side trim piece, it measures about 4 feet 1½ inches because the trim has been allowed to hang over. Notice a trim piece at the back of the unit just under the lid. Screws will be driven through it and into wall studs to keep the unit from falling over.

For interior shelves, consider using little clips that simply slip into holes drilled on cabinet sides. Above the round peg, these clips feature a flat ledge on which shelves can rest. Use a piece of pegboard as a template for drilling holes. Be certain your pegboard template is positioned exactly the same each time so that holes are aligned on both cabinet sides.

Interior shelves

Installation

A furring strip was secured to the wall to compensate for part of a concrete foundation that juts into the garage at the floor level. Furring was cut just as wide as the concrete. Cabinets will rest against the concrete foundation and furring strip at the same time to remain vertically upright and plumb. Furring was placed at the same level as the cabinet's rear, upper inside trim piece. Screws will be driven through the cabinet's upper rear trim piece, through the furring, and into studs.

Countertops

Counters are cut and assembled the same as cabinets. Side panels are grooved so that plywood shelves can slip into them for a tight and secure fit. Both horizontal and vertical trim pieces are positioned with open toe areas in front and are covered in back with ¼-inch hardboard. Countertops are reinforced with 2 × 4s as a means to support weight on them. These units will be covered with ACX plywood then with a sheet of laminate.

Top counter corners are reinforced with wood blocks. Blocks are glued and then screwed in place. Screws were driven from the inside. Use caution to avoid driving screws through counter fronts. Screws must be inserted at an angle. Bar clamps do an excellent job of holding 2-x-4 reinforcement boards in place while the boards are screwed in place. Screws are inserted high on face pieces so that trim attached to the plywood top's edge can hide them. Horizontal plywood strips at the top and lower shelf serve as backing supports. Hardboard will be nailed to them.

When the two modules are positioned against the wall, you can see that an air space exists between them. The units are flush at their front trim pieces. Once they were set plumb and level, a screw was driven from one plywood panel into the other to hold them steady while they were screwed to studs in the wall behind.

Upper cupboards are built and secured to walls like cabinets. Note the space between these units as viewed from underneath. By looking at the front trim pieces, you could never tell they were separated. Side trim pieces are fastened together with screws. Drill a pilot hole first to avoid splitting trim.

This cupboard is the last in line. Its outside face is clearly visible. Because of this, side trim was held back to just ⅛ of an inch overhang. An attractive piece of ⅛-inch wood veneer was then glued to the cupboard's side panel flush with the trim. As viewed from underneath, you can see how the trim is designed to hang over and hide cupboard bottoms.

There are a number of different ways to make drawers. Fine woodworking craftspeople make furniture drawers with intricate dovetail joints and spend hours detailing their work to pure excellence. Others simply nail together a few boards into the shape of a box with no lid and call it a day.

One of the easiest and efficient ways to make drawers is with plywood sides and a hardboard bottom. The ends of both ¾-inch ACX plywood sides have been grooved (rabbeted) with a ¾-inch rabbet-router bit. Fronts were screwed and glued to them. Before they were put together, a ¼-inch groove was cut along the bottom of all four pieces to secure the hardwood bottom.

A front or back was first glued and screwed to the side panels, then the bottom hardwood piece was slipped into position. Next, the fourth plywood piece was attached. A separate piece of hardwood plywood was rabbeted and secured to the front plywood piece to serve as an actual face front. Drawer fronts are secured to drawer front pieces with screws no longer than 1⅛ inch so that they do not protrude from the nice drawer face. Handles are then installed with their screws, helping to keep drawer faces secure.

The ¾-inch-thick, 2-inch-wide trim around the top edge of this counter has been covered with laminate glued in place. Notice that drawer faces actually slip in the drawer openings by about ⅜ of an inch. This is accomplished by rabbeting drawer face edges.

Openings for drawers can be made to any size you desire. However, once the counter is built, you have to make sure that drawer dimensions are built to take into account the specifications designated on the drawer guides or rollers you plan to use. The directions for side-mounted drawer guides state that the drawer width must be at least ½-inch narrower than the counter opening width. This accounts for the width of guide hardware. Pay strict attention to the directions for drawer guides. Drawers made just 1/16 of an inch too wide will be hard to pull out and push in. Drawers made too narrow will wobble from side to side each time they are operated.

Cabinet and cupboard finishing

To ensure tight-fitting and long-lasting wood joints, apply wood glue to all joints first before driving nails or wood screws. Wipe off excess glue that seeps out from joints with a clear water-moistened rag.

Cabinet trim does not look nearly as appealing with nail heads in plain view as it does when nails are set and their holes are filled with wood putty.

Set nails about 1/16 inch to a maximum of ⅛ inch deep into the wood. As a quick fix, dab a bit of wood glue over holes, let it set for a few minutes, then sand the area all around, including the nail holes. Sanding dust will combine with the wood glue to make repairs nearly invisible. In lieu of this method and for more permanent finishing, use a wood putty designed for the type of wood you're using.

Nothing finishes off a quality cabinet, cupboard, or counter unit like sanding. Makita offers a wide range of sanders in both cordless and corded models. Belt sanders work fast to smooth out rough surfaces. Finishing sanders are more gentle. When used according to directions, wood is sanded to a fine ultra-smooth perfection.

Although wood putty and sanding go a long way toward hiding nails, at times there is just no way to adequately hide them because the wood grain is impossible to match. Even then, properly filled, sanded, and stained cabinets will look great despite a few nail-set images that are vaguely visible.

Cabinet, cupboard, and counter doors do a great job of hiding all of the household junk that mysteriously finds its way out into the garage or workshop.

For woodworking shops, I encourage you to rabbet all door edges to help keep sawdust and other debris out of storage spaces. Rabbeted door edges require specially designed hinges. Stanley offers a number of different styles.

It is easiest to attach cabinet, cupboard, and counter doors while units are loose and not yet secured to walls. Lay units on their backs so that the doors lie flat.

Cut doors 1 inch wider and 1 inch longer than their openings. Rabbet door edges ⅜ of an inch deep and ½ inch wide. To ensure

a ½-inch width, take your time in adjusting your router's guide. Use a piece of scrap wood to test your measurements before actually going after the doors. Top hinge edges are normally set about 4 inches down from the top, and bottom hinge edges are set about 4 inches up from the bottom of cabinet and cupboard doors. Place the doors upside down on cabinets and cupboards, make your 4-inch marks, then position the hinges.

The hinges will be screwed to the backsides of doors first. Use a screw set to accurately make a pilot hole for the first screw before you drive it in. Once the first screw has been set, check the hinge to make sure it has not moved and is still in its correct position. Then set the second and third screws. Attach hinges to the backs of all doors.

With all the hinges attached to the doors, turn the doors back over to their correct position. Take your time positioning doors so they rest in the center of their openings and are in line with doors above and below them. After you confirm they are correctly positioned, set hinges to trim. Use the screw set to make a pilot hole. Unless you made a mistake in positioning the door, your door should look straight, level, plumb, and perpendicular. Handles are fastened by drilling holes completely through doors and then inserting screws into them from door backs.

Once your cabinets and counters have been sanded, sealed, and stained, finish them with cove molding or wood trim. Cabinets, cupboards, and counters built like these will make your workshop look clean, crisp, organized, and very well managed.

Workshop amenities

YOUR HOME workshop should be set up and outfitted the way you want it. As long as everything in your work area is constructed safely, obstacles do not block work around power equipment, and electrical circuits are not overloaded, you can have anything in your workshop desired—even a kitchen sink!

It is common for active do-it-yourself home workshops to be filled with such things as a telephone, a sound system, a television set, a washroom, a refrigerator, chairs, a microwave oven, and other household conveniences. Before you finish off all the workshop walls, consider what types of amenities you might want someday and prepare for them. Think about installing wiring for a telephone, a sound system, or an intercom. Consider adding a water line for a refrigerator ice-maker, plumbing for a washroom, and so on.

If your shop is located away from the house, a workshop doorbell connected to the button at your home's front door can be a viable addition. When you are expecting a delivery of new tools or supplies, you will want to know when a delivery person has arrived.

General ideas

Because some shop equipment will make considerable noise, consider installing a loud bell or horn connected to the workshop telephone. The horn should be wired so that every time the phone rings the horn sounds. Equip the horn with a disconnect so that it won't startle you while working on intricate, noise-free projects. Many workshop owners install lights that flash brightly when someone rings a doorbell, the telephone rings, or a family member needs the attention of someone in the workshop.

Vacuum systems

A central vacuum system could serve both your workshop and home. The best time to install plastic piping for such systems is while walls are open, and before insulation and drywall are applied. A power head unit might work best for home use. On the other hand, a simple vacuum hose and tool kit is ideal for workshops.

Forced air heat is not generally a good idea for active workshops where lots of airborne debris is created. Sawdust and similar products will find their way through ducting and into other rooms. However, a new living space above a new ground-level workshop will require heat ducting. Heat registers and ducting must be installed before you cover ceiling and wall spaces.

A refrigerator and telephone are located next to a sink counter in Jim Yocum's home garage/workshop. Fresh water and drain plumbing pipes are located in the wall behind. Utility sinks and faucets are easy to install. While contemplating outfitting your new workshop, be sure to plan for and run rough plumbing to places where such facilities ultimately will be located.

Workshop sinks

Installation instructions for our Kohler stainless steel sink and faucet were most informative. We began by placing the sink unit upside down on the counter, tracing its outline with a soft lead pencil, and then using a square to duplicate that tracing ¼ inch inside all lines. To make a ½-inch radius at the corners, I used a piece of ¾-inch copper pipe. A hole was drilled in the counter to make access for a jigsaw blade. The saw cut through the counter's laminate and particleboard top with ease.

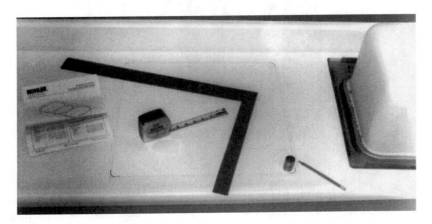

According to instructions, the sink's mounting clips were attached along featured rails all around the unit's bottom edge. A bead of DAP latex sealant was then run along the sink's entire bottom edge to prevent water from seeping into the counter's storage area.

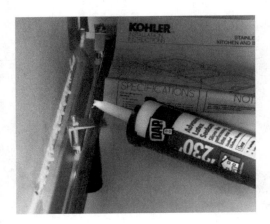

From underneath the countertop, you can see how clips hold this sink solidly in position. Notice some excess sealant at the top left. On the countertop surface, excess sealant was wiped away with a clean, dry cloth. NOTE: It is easier to assemble and install faucets before sinks are fastened to countertops.

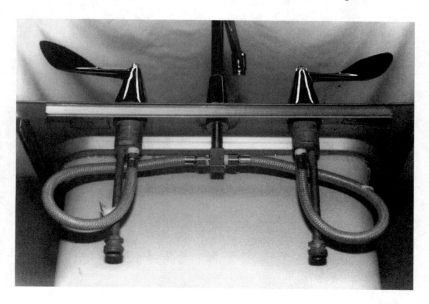

This Kohler faucet features a tall spigot that will make it easy to wash odd-shaped objects in the workshop's utility sink. Likewise, wrist-control handles were selected so that we can turn on water by using our wrists instead of our soiled hands. For new sinks, you will need to attach shut-off valves to the ½-inch copper, freshwater pipes that come out of the wall. The PlumbShop offers vanity installation kits that include two shutoffs, two hoses, copper pipe fittings, and Teflon pipe tape. Hoses connect directly to both shutoffs and faucets.

Workshop washrooms

Space heaters fit under counters at floor level. Toe space areas must allow at least a 3⅝-inch clearance from the floor to the bottom side of a counter's bottom shelf. NuTone offers these heaters in both 110-volt and 220-volt models. Workshop washrooms and small offices should be well served with heat. Consider a NuTone Kickspace Heater for them.

If your workshop is physically big enough, consider adding a washroom for those times when you find yourself covered with sawdust, grease, or other stuff not allowed in the house.

Closet flanges are available in 3- and 4-inch sizes, and they attach directly to 3- or 4-inch sewer lines. Wide heads on

special toilet-mounting screws are inserted into closet-flange grooves. Screw stems then stick up through toilet bases and are secured with nuts. Connections from toilets to closet flanges are made watertight with wax rings. A PlumbShop toilet installation kit included a wax ring and all the parts needed to connect our Kohler toilet to fresh water.

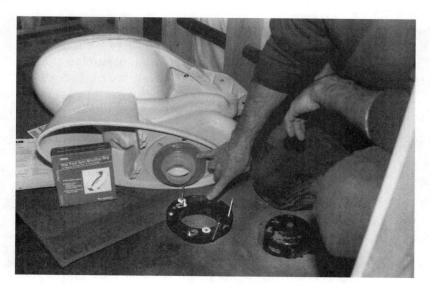

Toilet tanks are secured to bowls with bolts. A rubber gasket maintains a watertight seal. This low water-use Kohler toilet came packaged with all the parts necessary to completely assemble the unit. The PlumbShop toilet installation kit provided all of the parts needed to make brand new connections from the ½-inch copper, freshwater supply pipe to the toilet tank.

Toilets are not installed until after drywall is finished. For illustrative purposes, this photograph shows how a freshwater pipe is stubbed out of the wall. Note the main drainpipe stack behind the toilet to which this toilet's drain is connected below the concrete floor surface.

The toilet's freshwater copper pipe is cut to the desired length and then outfitted with a shut-off valve. A flexible hose is then connected to the shutoff and run to the bottom of the toilet tank. Most toilet tanks feature their fresh water inlets on the left side as you stand in front of them.

Bathroom fans make nice additions. They are required for all bathrooms equipped with showers or bathtubs as a means of removing moisture from those spaces. This NuTone model features a regular light and night-light. Notice the fan ducting

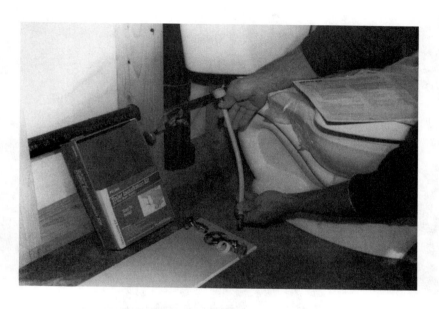

Workshop amenities   109

that exits above the bathroom window. A wall cap equipped with a hinged door is scheduled for installation on the exterior wall through the rim joist block. A unit that includes separate switches for the lights and a timer for the fan will be mounted on the wall next to the bathroom door.

Showers If you plan to install a shower unit in your workshop's washroom, be sure to provide an entry point wide enough for such a unit to fit through. An opening was left in our workshop's washroom exterior wall for just this reason. Shower units are large and inflexible. You might have to temporarily knock out a wall stud for shower-stall access.

To facilitate this shower's installation, a rear wall was purposely left out; it will be built after the shower is positioned. Ground-level showers must be provided a drain at floor level. This drain runs under the concrete floor to a sewer line below. Shower-drain fittings are available at home-improvement centers and plumbing supply houses.

According to installation instructions, position your shower stall over the drain, and make sure studs are provided along the stall's front nailing flanges. If no studs are located in those positions, you will have to put them in. Pull stalls out of the way to install nailing-flange studs and make sure all wall insulation is properly secured.

With these preparations complete, position the stall in place and make the required drain connection. Drill pilot holes along

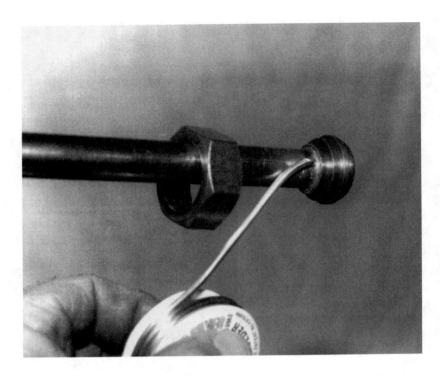

the front nailing flanges, 8 inches on center, and around the top of the stall at each stud. Be certain that the unit rests plumb and level. Use shims under them as necessary. Attach shower stalls to studs with screws.

Once the shower stalls have been positioned securely, work can begin on the faucets. Our Kohler faucet system came complete with all fittings and connections. Before sweating on copper pipe to faucet fittings, be sure faucet nuts have been slipped onto pipes. It is these nuts that will hold hot- and cold-water pipes to the faucet.

To sweat on copper connections to copper pipe, you must first clean the pipe end and interior sleeve of the fitting with emery cloth. Don't skimp on this procedure. Make copper shine like new. Then, apply flux to both the pipe end and fitting sleeve, fit them together, and heat up the fitting. Do not heat the pipe. When flux starts boiling, gently apply solder and watch it melt

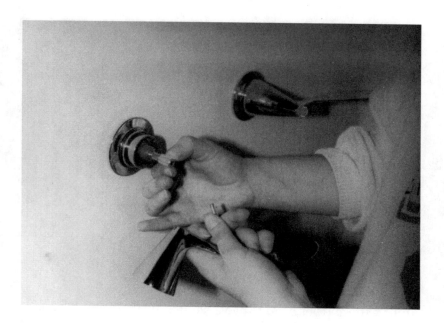

right into the fitting sleeve. Wipe off excess solder with a soaking wet rag.

A small hole was first drilled through the shower stall to designate where one faucet outlet would poke through. A faucet template was then taped in place with one hole fitted right over the hole drilled in the stall. This allowed us to properly position holes for both the hot- and cold-water faucets. The faucet was installed according to directions, and wrist-control handle positions were adjusted evenly through their specially grooved fittings.

A single, upright ½-inch copper pipe was attached to the faucet unit and routed upward to where we wanted the shower head positioned. A special elbow fitting equipped with threads on one end was sweated onto this pipe. A hole was drilled through the shower stall at that elbow to make room for the shower head arm. The threaded arm end was wrapped with Teflon pipe tape then screwed into the threaded elbow fitting. Teflon pipe thread was then wrapped around the other end of the shower arm and the head was screwed on. Masking tape was wrapped

around the shower head to avoid scratching its fine polished surface with a wrench.

While installing your shower unit, take care to prevent unnecessary damage to any component. This stall was lined with cardboard to ensure ladder legs would not scratch the floor of the shower.

To install water-resistant drywall, first nail furring strips on studs to compensate for the ⅛-inch distance that the shower-stall nailing flanges protrude. Masking tape marks each stud location so that the studs will be easy to find while driving drywall screws.

Next, run a bead of sealant along the stall's nailing flanges. Drywall edges will make contact with the flanges to ensure a tight fit. After the drywall is completely finished, fill any gaps between the drywall and the base of the stall's nailing flanges with another bead of sealant. The sealant prevents moisture from being wicked up and into the ends of drywall.

Water-resistant drywall was cut in such a way that paper-wrapped edges were placed on top of the stall. Freshly cut edges that expose inner drywall material were placed at the ceiling level. This is a recommended installation maneuver. Paper-wrapped drywall edges are many times more moisture resistant than fresh-cut exposed edges.

Drywall work on the other side of our shower wall presented a few problems because of pipes and the lack of support for drywall edges. In lieu of studs or other wood drywall nailing blocks, I installed a few Simpson drywall stops. Installed correctly, drywall stops support drywall edges in those spaces that lack any other means of support. In this corner, the first piece of drywall to go up will be the one that goes over the drywall stops. This way, a perpendicular piece on the other wall can butt against it to further hold it secure in the corner.

Drywall

Summary

Home workshops undergo lots of subtle changes over the years. You will most likely learn better ways to achieve various projects with tools and equipment arranged differently than originally planned. Because avid do-it-yourselfers have a knack for always striving to improve things, don't short-change yourself now by limiting the overall and long-term possibilities for your shop. Plan for the future by providing your shop with rough plumbing, a more-than-adequate electrical system, and convenience items like speaker wire that can always be hooked up later.

Never get into a hurry. Take your time and change those things—such as electrical outlets, wall switches, light fixtures, and so on—you notice need changing. Once your workshop has been finished with a wall covering and you have started moving in, adding structural components will be more difficult and time-consuming to accomplish.

Tool and equipment attributes

To ACCOMPLISH ANYTHING in a workshop, you need tools to work with. Although many professional workshops are used by people who must work to earn a living, most of us do-it-yourselfers regard our workshops as friendly places where we can putter, tinker, relax, and enjoy ourselves. Although we expect to accomplish some work in our workshops, we are always on the lookout for tools and accessories to make our jobs easier.

All the tools and accessories described in this chapter are available through the companies listed in the Sources at the end of the book. I encourage you to contact them for catalogs and more information.

Because of a number of different factors, it took a while for our workshop to finally be served with its own lights. In the meantime, halogen lights like this one from Harbor Freight Tools allowed us to work in the shop during darkness. An electrical receptacle mounted on the light's stand came in handy for charging our cordless tools.

You can almost never have enough light in your workshop. This is a multipurpose incandescent light unit from The Eastwood Company. It comes with magnetic and clamp bases. Use such a light for close-up electronics work, appliance repair, model building, power equipment precision use, and anything else where lighting is a concern.

Lighting

Ladders To install light fixtures, electrical wires, insulation, and drywall, you'll need ladders. This Articulated Ladder from Keller Ladders works great. It can be adjusted to a number of different positions for all types of applications. Here, I used one side of the ladder to work on one end of a light and the other side for the other. I didn't need two ladders nor did I have to move one around each time I needed to get to the far end of a light fixture.

Saws We put our Makita Hypoid Saw to the test during workshop construction and it still cuts like a champ. Here, a Multipurpose Guide from Harbor Freight Tools is set up to guide the saw along an 8 foot length of plywood. Notice that two 2×4s are on each side of the proposed cut. This method is ideal for cutting plywood. The guide helps saws cut straight and the 2×4s keep both plywood sides supported during and after cuts.

Drills

Drilling through all these 2-x-6 Glu-Lam supports would have been impossible without extensions for Makita's Self-Drive Bits. First, I used the bit alone to get through the first stud. I then attached the 12-inch extension. It could not make it all the way through so I attached the 18-inch extension to the bit, fed it through as far as it would go, attached the extension to the ½ inch Angle Drill chuck, plugged the drill back in, and completed the hole.

You have to remember to pull Self-Feed Bits out of holes after they have bored about ¼ inch. If you don't, wood chips will compress in the holes making it almost impossible to pull bits out.

Bench top tools

If your workshop is a place where the family participates together in making and fixing things, you might consider benchtop tools designed for craft projects, such as a scroll saw and belt/disc sander. These units are from Harbor Freight Tools. We expect to get a lot of use out of them, especially when Christmas approaches.

No workbench is complete without a vise. With a couple of exceptions, most are from Harbor Freight Tools. On the left is a heavy-duty woodworker vise. Next to it are Vise-Grip Hold-Down Clamps fastened to the bench with long screw mounts, a washer, and a wing nut. In the center is a huge vise most appropriate for an all-around workbench. An anvil on the back offers a good place for pounding on metal things. Next to it is a Stanley woodworker vise complete with hardwood lined jaws.

Vise

Tool and equipment attributes   121

At the far right is a small utility vise perfect for this size workbench. On the shelf below is an assortment of hardwood woodworking clamps.

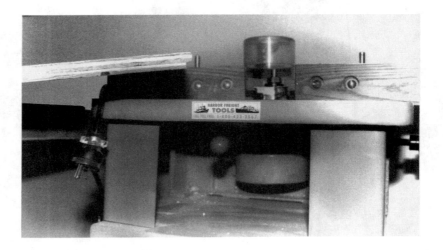

Router

Many do-it-yourself woodworkers have successfully shaped lots of wood projects using a router and/or router table. Essentially, a powerful router mounted on a heavy-duty stand, make shapers exceptionally quick work of putting all sorts of edges on wood. A variety of shaper bits allow users to make molding, trim, and other shapes with ease. This unit is set up to rabbet and round off edges of ¾-inch plywood cabinet doors, all in one pass. Practice with shapers is mandatory. It takes a while to accurately set them up, so have plenty of scrap wood on hand. Once properly adjusted, your shaping jobs can be completed in no time.

Drill press

A drill press is basically a power drill mounted inside an unmovable housing. Everything you drill with this tool will be perfect. A drill press is ideal for those home improvement jobs where numerous holes must be drilled at even increments and even depths. Here, the machine is set up for drilling plugs. Plugs are perfectly cylindrical chunks of wood designed that fit inside holes bored for screws. Plugs fit over screws to make assemblies look as though nothing holds them together.

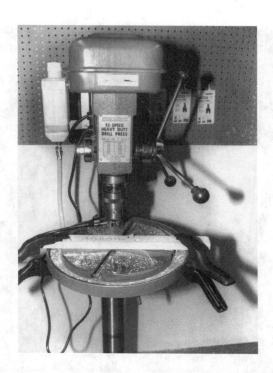

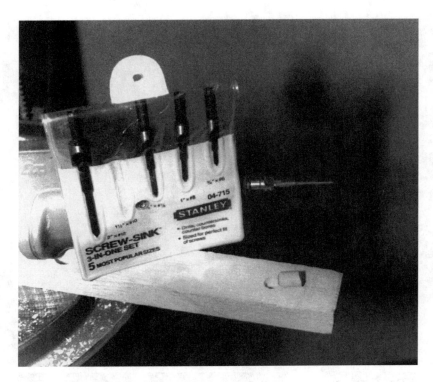

Screw-sink drill bits bore pilot holes for screws, and countersink and counterbore holes for screws. After screws have been driven into wood to the point where their head is below the surface, plugs are inserted and then sanded flush with wood surfaces for blemish-free finishes.

Compressed air

Luke and Nick are draining moisture from the tanks on our portable Campbell Hausfeld Air Compressor. Small 1 horsepower and 1.5 horsepower units like these are perfect for jobs inside and outside the workshop where compressed air power is needed for pneumatic staplers, nailers, and finish nailers. This unit has been used to staple sheathing, nail studs, affix cedar shakes, fill car tires, and numerous other tasks. It's quiet and efficient.

For our overall home workshop and garage needs, we selected a Campbell Hausfeld 5 horsepower, 60 gallon air compressor. Before you insulate and apply drywall to your workshop walls, consider

the benefits of a complete compressed air system piped throughout your workshop. Do-it-yourselfers and professionals alike have both experienced success with compressed air systems served by appropriate high, psi-rated PVC plastic pipe, copper pipe, and black pipe. The choice is yours. Connect your compressor's outlet to the main wall mount with rubber hose so vibration from the unit will not transfer to walls, which will eventually loosen mounting bolts and other connections. Run piping downhill to a dryer so moisture condensation is easily trapped before it gets to your tools.

On the wall to the right of the compressor is a Campbell Hausfeld regulator and automatic oiler. A special female connection is featured at the regulator. This is designed exclusively for spray painting lines. Oilers are designed to lubricate pneumatic staplers, nailers, grinders, and other comparable tools. Spray paint guns must have pure, clean compressed air. Oil in gun lines will quickly ruin paint jobs.

Workshops served by main air compressor units should be outfitted with numerous outlets. In addition to plentiful workbench connections, don't overlook ceiling mounts. You never know when compressed air will come in handy in the middle of your workshop. Likewise, an outlet located close to your home's garage doors could prove handy for filling car tires.

Dust collector Airborne particles and sawdust can be harmful to people and equipment and tools. This dust collector system from Makita gathers an unbelievable amount of sawdust. Clean sawdust and wood shavings can be spread around your garden and flower beds instead of just tossing them in the trash.

In addition to serving as a worthy sawdust collector, a dust collector system is quickly converted to a blower. It works fast to blow away sawdust and other light debris from equipment, tools, and items hanging on pegboard.

By all means, look forward to outfitting your workshop with lots of handy tools, pieces of equipment, and gadgets of all types. The more you can do to make your workshop environment more comfortable, the more time you and your family will spend fixing things, making gifts, learning about tools and home components, and having a good time.

I hope the information in this book helps you and your family put together a first-class and productive workshop. Remember to abide by all of the safety recommendations mentioned in this book and those provided with all the installation and operating instruction manuals that accompany the products you purchase and tools and equipment you use. Best wishes to you and your family as you work together in your home workshop.

Numerous pieces of literature and products featured throughout this book were selected by me and my family from the companies and associations listed below. Those items of interest that we used for our various projects were hand picked because of their quality and the customer service we received from their manufacturers and suppliers. I recommend you contact these companies for further information about their products, plans, informative literature, and other information that might be available.

American Plywood Association
PO Box 11700
Tacoma, WA 98411
(206) 565-6600
Information and building plans for plywood.

Autodesk Retail Products
11911 North Creek Parkway South
Bothell, WA 98011
(800) 228-3601

American Tool Companies, Inc.
PO Box 337
De Witt, NE 68341
(402) 683-2315
Vise-Grips, Quick-Grips, Prosnip, CHESCO, and more.

Alta Industries
PO Box 2764
Santa Rosa, CA 95405
(707) 544-5009
Tool belts and pouches.

Behr Process Corporation
3400 West Segerstrom Avenue
Santa Ana, CA 92704
(800) 854-0133
Paint, stain, varnish, and sealers.

Campbell Hausfeld
100 Production Drive
Harrison, OH 45030
(513) 367-4811

Compressed-air equipment and tools.

Cedar Shake and Shingle Bureau
515 - 116th Avenue NE, Suite 275
Bellevue, WA 98004-5294
(206) 453-1323

Information regarding cedar shakes and shingles.

DAP, Inc.
PO Box 277
Dayton, OH 45401
(800) 568-4554

Sealants, caulking, adhesives, and a lot more.

Eagle Windows and Doors
375 East Ninth Street
Dubuque, IA 52004
(319) 556-2270

Wood windows and doors.

The Eastwood Company
580 Lancaster Avenue, Box 3014
Malvern, PA 19355-0714
(800) 345-1178

Huge selection of automotive and workshop tools and supplies.

Empire Brush, Inc.
U.S. 13 North
PO Box 1606
Greenville, NC 27835-1606
(919) 758-4111

Brushes, brooms, and accessories of all kinds.

Freud
PO Box 7187
High Point, NC 27264
(800) 472-7307

Power tools.

General Cable Company (Romex™)
4 Tesseneer Drive
Highland Heights, KY 41076
(606) 572-8000

Electrical wire of all kinds.

Häfele America Co.
3901 Cheyenne Drive
P.O. Box 4000
Archdale, NC 27263
(910) 889-2322

Cabinet hardware of all kinds.

Halo Lighting, Brand of Copper Lighting
400 Bussey Road
Elk Grove Village, IL 60007
(708) 956-8400

Recessed ceiling lights.

Harbor Freight Tools (Central Purchasing, Inc.)
3491 Mission Oaks Boulevard
Camarillo, CA 95008
(800) 423-2567

Tools, supplies, and products for every workshop.

Kohler Company
444 Highland Drive
Kohler, WI 53044
(414) 457-4441

Bathroom fixtures of all kinds.

Keller Ladders
18000 State Road Nine
Miami, FL 33162
(800) 222-2600

Ladders of all kinds.

Leviton Manufacturing Company, Inc.
59-25 Little Neck Parkway
Little Neck, NY 11362-2591
(718) 229-4040

Electrical switches, receptacles, and a lot more.

Leslie-Locke, Inc.
4501 Circle 75 Parkway, Suite F-6300
Atlanta, GA 30339
Roof windows, skylights, and a lot more.

Makita U.S.A., Inc.
14930 Northam Street
La Mirada, CA 90638-5753
(714) 522-8088
Cordless and power tools of all kinds.

McGuire-Nicholas Company, Inc.
2331 Tubeway Avenue
City of Commerce, CA 90040
(213) 722-6961
Tool belts, pouches, knee pads, back braces, and more.

NuTone
Madison and Red Bank Roads
Cincinnati, OH 45227-1599
(800) 543-8687
Built-in convenience products.

Owens-Corning Fiberglas Insulation
Fiberglas Tower
Toledo, OH 43659
(800) 342-3745
Insulation for ceilings, floors, and walls.

PanelLift Telpro, Inc.
Route 1, Box 138
Grand Forks, ND 58201
(800) 441-0551
Drywall lift equipment.

PlumbShop (a division of Brass-Craft)
39600 Orchard Hill Place
Novi, MI 48376
(810) 305-6000
Plumbing supplies.

Plano Molding Company
431 East South Street
Plano, IL 60545-1601
(800) 874-6905

Plastic tool boxes, storage units, shelves, and more.

Power Products Company—SIMKAR
Cayuga and Ramona Streets
Philadelphia, PA 19120
(800) 346-7833

Fluorescent lighting for all applications.

Power Tool Institute, Inc.
1300 Sumner Avenue
Cleveland, OH 44115-2851
(216) 241-7333

Information about the safe use of power tools.

Simpson Strong-Tie Company, Inc.
1450 Doolittle Drive
San Leandro, CA 94577
(800) 999-5099

Metal connectors for every building requirement and more.

The Stanley Works
1000 Stanley Drive
New Britain, CT 06053
(800) 551-5936

Hand tools, hardware, closet organizers, and a lot more.

Sta-Put Color Pegs
23504 - 29th Avenue West
Lynnwood, WA 98036-8318

Colored plastic pegboard hooks that always stay put.

Structron Corporation
1980 Diamond Street
San Marcos, CA 92069
(619) 744-6371

Garden and construction tools: shovels, rakes, brooms, etc.

Tyvek Housewrap (DuPont, Inc.)
Chestnut Run WR-2058
Wilmington, DE 19880-0722
(800) 448-9835
Exterior house wrap.

U.S. Ceramic, Co.
10233 Sandyville Road SE
East Sparta, OH 44626
(216) 866-5531
All kinds of ceramic tile.

Weiser Lock
6660 South Broadmoor Road
Tucson, AZ 85746
(602) 741-6200
Door locks, handles, and knobs.

Western Wood Products Association
522 SW Fifth Avenue
Portland, OR 97204-2122
(503) 224-3930
Information and lots of building plans for wood.

Zircon Corporation
1580 Dell Avenue
Campbell, CA 95008
(408) 866-8600
Water levels and other devices.

Other Bestsellers of Related Interest

Home Storage: Projects for Every Room
—*David H. Jacobs, Jr.*
Perfect for anyone who wants to maximize space, this book teaches how to make use of space under stairways, in attics, basements, and other areas. Includes tips on reorganizing existing storage areas. Installation and building instructions provided.
Paper $14.95, ISBN 0-07-032404-2

Home Improvement Tools and Equipment
—*David H. Jacobs, Jr.*
The perfect do-it-yourselfer's quick-reference to woodworking tools and accessories. Contains helpful guidelines for selecting hand and power tools, as well as routine maintenance and repair procedures.
Paper $14.95, ISBN 0-8306-4420-2

Workshops & Outbuildings
—*David H. Jacobs, Jr.*
Low-cost backyard building techniques for woodworkers. Includes design plans and step-by-step, illustrated instructions for building storage sheds, workshops, detached garages, hobby retreats, and more.
Paper $14.95, ISBN 0-8306-4421-0

24 Router Projects, 2nd Edition
—Percy W. Blandford
A collection of inexpensive projects that make the most of the router's workshop potential. Includes easy-to-follow, illustrated instructions for making kitchen accessories, furniture, cabinets, and more.
Paper $12.95, ISBN 0-8306-4546-2